Timothy O'Connell

Self-Concept and Adventure Education

A Study of Adolescents Engaged in Outdoor Adventure Activities

VDM Verlag Dr. Müller

Impressum/Imprint (nur für Deutschland/ only for Germany)

Bibliografische Information der Deutschen Nationalbibliothek: Die Deutsche Nationalbibliothek verzeichnet diese Publikation in der Deutschen Nationalbibliografie; detaillierte bibliografische Daten sind im Internet über http://dnb.d-nb.de abrufbar.

Alle in diesem Buch genannten Marken und Produktnamen unterliegen warenzeichen-, marken- oder patentrechtlichem Schutz bzw. sind Warenzeichen oder eingetragene Warenzeichen der jeweiligen Inhaber. Die Wiedergabe von Marken, Produktnamen, Gebrauchsnamen, Handelsnamen, Warenbezeichnungen u.s.w. in diesem Werk berechtigt auch ohne besondere Kennzeichnung nicht zu der Annahme, dass solche Namen im Sinne der Warenzeichen- und Markenschutzgesetzgebung als frei zu betrachten wären und daher von jedermann benutzt werden dürften.

Coverbild: www.purestockx.com

Verlag: VDM Verlag Dr. Müller Aktiengesellschaft & Co. KG
Dudweiler Landstr. 99, 66123 Saarbrücken, Deutschland
Telefon +49 681 9100-698, Telefax +49 681 9100-988, Email: info@vdm-verlag.de
Zugl.: New York, New York University, Diss., 2001

Herstellung in Deutschland:
Schaltungsdienst Lange o.H.G., Berlin
Books on Demand GmbH, Norderstedt
Reha GmbH, Saarbrücken
Amazon Distribution GmbH, Leipzig
ISBN: 978-3-639-17520-2

Imprint (only for USA, GB)

Bibliographic information published by the Deutsche Nationalbibliothek: The Deutsche Nationalbibliothek lists this publication in the Deutsche Nationalbibliografie; detailed bibliographic data are available in the Internet at http://dnb.d-nb.de.

Any brand names and product names mentioned in this book are subject to trademark, brand or patent protection and are trademarks or registered trademarks of their respective holders. The use of brand names, product names, common names, trade names, product descriptions etc. even without a particular marking in this works is in no way to be construed to mean that such names may be regarded as unrestricted in respect of trademark and brand protection legislation and could thus be used by anyone.

Cover image: www.purestockx.com

Publisher:
VDM Verlag Dr. Müller Aktiengesellschaft & Co. KG
Dudweiler Landstr. 99, 66123 Saarbrücken, Germany
Phone +49 681 9100-698, Fax +49 681 9100-988, Email: info@vdm-publishing.com
New York, New York University, Diss., 2001

Printed in the U.S.A.
Printed in the U.K. by (see last page)
ISBN: 978-3-639-17520-2

TABLE OF CONTENTS

CHAPTER I

THE RESEARCH OBJECTIVE

With the goal of educating the "whole" student, including a student's self-concept and self-esteem, schools are searching for and initiating programs and activities to enhance self-concept (i.e., the perceptions one holds about him or herself), especially with adolescents (Shavelson, Hubner, & Stanton, 1976; Neill, 1997). Many of these programs designed to increase self-concept are offered for adolescents in the context of traditional academic settings such as high schools and colleges (Finkenberg, Shows & DiNucci, 1994; Gillett, Thomas, Skok, & McLaughlin, 1991; Kaplan, 1974; Lambert, Segger, Staley, Spencer & Nelson, 1978; Wilgenbush & Merrill, 1999). Additionally, programs specifically aimed at increasing the self-concept of youth at risk, adjudicated youth, females, people with disabilities, traditional high school students, and members of various minority groups have been implemented and studied. These programs have used a number of approaches based on several theoretical models that affect adolescent self-concept, and research studying the outcomes of these programs has reported mixed results (Hattie, Marsh, Neill & Richards, 1997; Hazelworth & Wilson, 1990; Luckner, 1989; Marsh & Richards, 1988; Marsh, Richards & Barnes, 1986, 1987; McDonald & Howe, 1989; Minor & Elrod, 1994; Neill; Rawson & McIntosh, 1991; Wilgenbush & Merrill).

Theoretical Rationale

Contemporary models of adolescent self-concept postulate that self-concept changes as a result of an individual's interaction with and reaction to context-based environmental conditions and is learned through these interactions (Bracken, 1992, 1996; Purkey, 1988; Shavelson, Hubner, & Stanton, 1976). Additionally, the interactions and outcomes may occur in one of several domains of self-concept related to the context-based environment. Bracken (1992) has identified these domains as: social self-concept (interactions with others), competence self-concept (success or failure in completing activities), affect self-concept (evaluation of validity of previous behaviors), academic self-concept (school-related achievements and interactions), family self-concept (relationships with family unit), and physical self-concept (physical ability and attributes).

An individual in a specific environment receives feedback, both from the self and from others as to his or her abilities and performance in each of these domains. The individual uses a variety of standards in which to measure this feedback; and specific domains of self-concept related to that environment are enhanced or decreased based on this comparison (Bracken, 1992; Marsh, 1989). The change to global self-concept will most likely occur as a result of changes to one or

1

more of the domains of self-concept. Additionally, changes to one domain of self-concept may affect another domain (e.g., positive change to social self-concept is transferred to beliefs about an individual's relationship with family members resulting in increased family self-concept) (Bracken, 1996). Self-concept programs that offer activities that challenge individuals and provide immediate, positive feedback may enhance self-concept (Hattie, et al., 1997; Marsh; Priest, 1993). Outdoor adventure education courses provide challenge and immediate, positive feedback and may augment adolescent self-concept.

There has been an increase in the number of outdoor adventure education programs in recent years, many of which have the main goal of improving the participants' self-concept (Hattie, et al., 1997; Neill, 1997). Outdoor adventure education programs use experiential activities such as backpacking, rock climbing, canoeing, and other outdoor recreation activities to achieve various goals and objectives. Previous researchers have investigated the effects of outdoor adventure education programs on the self-concept of youth at risk, adjudicated youth, people with disabilities, and youth participating in extended (21 day or more) experiences (Hattie et al.; Hazelworth & Wilson, 1990; Luckner, 1989; Marsh & Richards, 1988; Marsh, Richards & Barnes, 1986, 1987; McDonald & Howe, 1989; Minor & Elrod, 1994; Neill; Rawson & McIntosh, 1991). However, as the implementation and popularity of these self-concept enhancing programs continues to increase, there has been much controversy regarding the impact and efficacy of these programs. There has been particular debate on the differing effects of these programs on males and females (Wilgenbush & Merrill, 1999). Additionally, the research methods used to examine these programs and the changes in self-concept have been questioned (Hattie, et al., 1997).

Adolescence is a time of transition during the human lifespan. It is frequently divided into three stages: early, middle, and late adolescence. Middle adolescence coincides roughly with the high school years. The developmental tasks facing individuals during middle adolescence include: becoming physically self-reliant, achieving psychological autonomy from parents and other adults, expanding peer relationships, achieving intimate friendships, and learning to handle relationships, dating and sexuality. Paralleling these tasks, as well as those achieved in early adolescence (i.e., concern with how one looks and using one's body and mind effectively), are beliefs related to various realms of self-concept (Kimmel & Weiner, 1995).

Contemporary beliefs regarding self-concept posit that as children age into adolescence their self-concept becomes increasingly more abstract and differentiated, moving from a general nature to include more specific domains of self-concept (Bracken, 1992; Crain & Bracken, 1994; Shavelson, Hubner, & Stanton, 1976). Therefore, it is in adolescence that individuals are able to ascertain the

2

difference between and among the various domains of self-concept, making them a suitable population to study.

Some studies examining self-concept enhancing programs for adolescents reported significant differences between males and females in change in self-concept (Crain & Bracken, 1994; Jackson, Hodge, & Ingram, 1994; Marsh, 1993; Widamen, MacMillan, Hemsley, Little, & Balow, 1992). Further, these authors indicated that traditional beliefs about differences in adolescent male and adolescent female self-concept were generally well founded (e.g., males have greater physical, affect, academic, and competence self-concept; females have greater social and family self-concept). Although there were differences in the magnitude of change by males and females, the change was generally positive for both groups. However, Crain and Bracken, Hattie et al., and Wilgenbush and Merrill (1999) found the differences between males and females to be small in nature.

The greatest changes in adolescent self-concept were reported to occur in specific domains of self-concept related to individual's perceptions of themselves in specific contexts such as physical activities or social settings (Crain & Bracken, 1994; Jackson, Hodge, & Ingram, 1994; Marsh, 1993; Widamen et al., 1992). These findings suggest that changes in the domains of self-concept as well as changes in global self-concept may be different for males and females, and should be examined to better understand the impact of programs intended to enhance self-concept. This is particularly important when examining programs serving both males and females.

Some studies examining self-concept and outdoor adventure education were based on primitive theoretical models of self-concept, had limited statistical power due to small sample sizes, used flawed statistical techniques, provided no control or comparison group, or ignored independent variables affecting the participants' self-concept (Crain & Bracken, 1994; Delugach, Bracken, Bracken, & Schicke, 1992; Harter, 1986; Hattie et al., 1997). Neill (1997) recognized several additional shortcomings of the existing research regarding outdoor adventure education, including improper generalization of results from one type of program to other programs (e.g., Outward Bound, traditionally a 21-day program designed to provide individual and group challenges using the outdoors as a medium, to traditional school programs), variable outcomes between programs of the same type (e.g., different Outward Bound schools), scarcity of research on non-Outward Bound programs, and lack of research on programs lasting less that 14 days.

Hence, the examination of short-term programs not associated with Outward Bound programs is needed. Further, the use of traditional high school students as research participants is needed as programs serving this population continue to grow in popularity (Neill, 1997).

3

Additionally, the use of variables such as previous experience with outdoor adventure activities, current life events that may affect self-concept (e.g., death of a parent/guardian, moving place of residence, poor academic performance), risk-taking behaviors, and perception of risk associated with outdoor adventure education activities is warranted.

Although selected findings from previous studies indicated some beneficial outcomes of the programs for the participants, overall they presented an unclear picture as to the effects of outdoor adventure education courses on adolescent self-concept. Consequently, further research is needed (Hattie, et al., 1997; Neill, 1997).

Therefore, this investigator examined the changes in self-concept of adolescents enrolled in outdoor adventure education courses offered at a traditional college preparatory high school and explored how gender influenced changes in specific domains of self-concept. A contemporary, hierarchical model of self-concept was used, which regards general self-concept as consisting of six domains: competence, affect, social, family, academic, and physical. It was predicted that the results of this study would endorse the use of outdoor adventure education courses as a means of successfully increasing the self-concept of adolescents, as well as strengthen the existing knowledge base regarding the outcomes of participation in outdoor adventure education courses. It was postulated that this information would assist education and recreation policy-makers, managers, and programming personnel in designing self-concept enhancing programs for adolescents.

Hypotheses

This investigator proposed that adolescents of high school ages participating in outdoor adventure education courses, including at least two overnight outdoor experiences, would have greater changes in self-concept than those students not participating in those courses. The following hypotheses were proposed:

H_1: Students participating in the outdoor adventure education courses would have greater positive change in general self-concept as measured by the Multidimensional Self-Concept Scale (MSCS) than students not participating in the outdoor adventure education courses.

H_2: Students participating in the outdoor adventure education courses would have greater positive changes in physical self-concept as measured by the MSCS than students not participating in the outdoor adventure education courses.

H_3: Students participating in the outdoor adventure education courses would have greater positive change in affect self-concept as measured by the MSCS than students not participating in the outdoor adventure education courses.

4

H_4: Students participating in the outdoor adventure education courses would have greater positive change in competence self-concept as measured by the MSCS than students not participating in the outdoor adventure education courses.

H_5: Students participating in the outdoor adventure education courses would have greater positive change in social self-concept as measured by the MSCS than students not participating in the outdoor adventure education courses.

H_6: Students participating in the outdoor adventure education courses would have greater positive change in family self-concept as measured by the MSCS than students not participating in the outdoor adventure education courses.

H_7: Students participating in the outdoor adventure education courses would have greater positive change in academic self-concept as measured by the MSCS than students not participating in the outdoor adventure education courses.

H_8: Female students participating in the outdoor adventure education courses would have greater positive change in physical, affect, academic, and competence self-concept as measured by the MSCS than male students participating in the outdoor adventure education courses.

H_9: Male students participating in the outdoor adventure education courses would have a greater positive change in social and family self-concept as measured by the MSCS than females participating in the outdoor adventure education courses.

Previous outdoor experience, perception of risk associated with outdoor activities, and current level of risk taking behavior as well as the corresponding MSCS score from the first data collection session were used as covariates as appropriate. Additionally, self-reported current life events were used to determine if any participant's self-concept is unduly influenced by factors that could possible affect self-concept occurring in everyday life (e.g. death of a parent, moving location of residence, facing peer pressure).

Definitions

In this study the following definitions were used:

Self-concept is "a multidimensional and context-dependent learned behavioral pattern that reflects an individual's evaluation of past behaviors and experiences, influences an individual's current behaviors, and predicts an individual's future behaviors" (Bracken, 1992, p. 10). In this study, global or general self-concept was defined as the total score derived from the sum of the

5

domain scores (Competence, Affect, Social, Family, Academic, Physical) as measured by the Multidimensional Self-Concept Scale (MSCS) (Bracken, 1992).

Competence self-concept refers to an adolescent's success or failure in completing activities and operating effectively in an environment. In this study, competence self-concept was defined as the total score derived from the MSCS items related to competence self-concept (i.e., C Scale, or items 26 through 50).

Affect self-concept refers to an adolescent's evaluation of previous behaviors and how the adolescent reacts to these evaluations of his or her behaviors. In this study, affect self-concept was defined as the total score derived from the MSCS items related to affect self-concept (i.e., AFF Scale, or items 51 through 75).

Social self-concept refers to interactions with others, as well as the adolescent's ability to obtain goals and objectives through interaction with others. In this study, social self-concept was defined as the total score derived from the MSCS items related to social self-concept (i.e., S Scale, or items 1 through 25).

Family self-concept refers to interactions, behaviors, and beliefs about an adolescent's family unit, including parents/guardians, foster parents, grandparents, siblings, etc. or any other living arrangement. In this study, family self-concept was defined as the total score derived from the MSCS items related to family self-concept (i.e., F Scale, or items 101 through 125).

Academic self-concept refers to an adolescent's academic achievement as well as behaviors and interactions in a school environment, including those interactions with other students, teachers, and administrators. In this study, academic self-concept was defined as the total score derived from the MSCS items related to academic self-concept (i.e., AC Scale, or items 76 through 100).

Physical self-concept refers to an adolescent's physical ability and attributes, as well as reaction to the comparison with other's physical ability and attributes. In this study, physical self-concept was defined as the total score derived from the MSCS items related to physical self-concept (i.e., P Scale, or items 126 through 150).

Outdoor adventure education is the use of the outdoors and activities related to the outdoors to promote excitement, challenge, and personal involvement in an environment different from that normally experienced by individuals (Ewert, 1989; Hattie, et al, 1997). In this study, outdoor adventure education was defined as the participation in either of two academic courses, one titled "Experiential Education," the other "Wilderness" at Friends Seminary (a private, college-preparatory high school in New York City) during the Fall 2000 school semester. Both courses included traditional classroom learning, "hands-on" classroom activities, and at least two overnight (3 days/2 nights) outdoor experiences (camping, rock climbing, sea kayaking or backpacking).

CHAPTER II

THE RELATED LITERATURE

The literature related to this study falls into two major categories: adolescent self-concept and outdoor adventure education. It is important to examine the history, structure, hierarchical nature, and development of adolescent self-concept. Additionally, factors such as gender and ethnicity need to be considered. The literature relating to outdoor adventure education examines the historical roots and theoretical bases for these types of programs.

Self-Concept

Self-concept has been extensively studied by researchers from a variety of fields and is one of the more popular topics of research in psychological studies today (Strein, 1998). Self-concept has been defined as "...the totality of a complex, organized, and dynamic system of learned beliefs, attitudes and opinions that each person holds to be true about his or her personal existence" (Purkey, 1988, p. 1). Self-concept and self-esteem have often been used as interchangeable terms, although each refers to something different. Self-esteem has been defined as "feelings of personal worth and level of satisfaction regarding one's self" (Purkey, p. 1), and has been considered a part of self-concept. Self-concept is thought to be organized in a consistent manner and remain relatively stable over time. Early theories regarding the organization of self-concept posited that self-concept was general in nature, referred to the whole self, and was unidimensional (Harter, 1986). Current theories of self-concept regard the construct as multidimensional and relating to specific facets of an individual's sense of self (Bracken, Bunch, Keith & Keith, 2000; Marsh, Parker, & Barnes, 1985; Shavelson, Hubner, & Stanton, 1976).

History of Self-Concept

William James was one of the first theorists to describe the self in an all-encompassing manner. He suggested the self was comprised of four components: body, social self, spiritual self, and ego. James' conception of the self was hierarchical in nature, with the bodily self forming the foundation and culminating with ego. His argument posited that the self is a continual series of thoughts, each building on a remembrance of previous thought. The self is thus a thought and relates to one's self-identity (James, 1983).

Cooley (1902) introduced the notion of the "looking glass self" in which an individual presents him or herself to others, forms a perception of how others see him or her, and uses that information as a representation of the self. The inclusion of social feedback and internalization of this feedback was an important contribution to self-concept history, and is tied to contemporary theories.

Theories of self-concept in the mid 1900's were based on the assumption that self-concept was unidimensional. It was believed that children and adolescents were not able to distinguish between the domains of self-concept (Harter, 1996). However, during the 1970s and 1980s researchers such as Shavelson, Hubner and Stanton (1976), Byrne and Shavelson (1987), and Marsh, Parker, and Barnes (1985) developed and exhaustively studied multidimensional, hierarchical models of self-concept that included both situation specific and general, or global domains. Additionally, contemporary researchers have refined these multidimensional, hierarchical models of self-concept and developed measurement instruments for use with today's children and adolescents (Bracken, 1992; Bracken et al. 2000).

Structure of Self-Concept

Three major characteristics of self-concept have been identified as important: 1) self-concept is learned, 2) self-concept is organized, and 3) self-concept is dynamic (Purkey, 1998). The development of self-concept is a learning process in which individuals are consistently engaged. The organizational aspects of self-concept suggest that individuals tend to resist change to their concepts of self. As self-concept is hierarchically organized, general self-concept remains more stable than its specific domains. The dynamic nature of self-concept guides individuals' perceptions of their roles in everyday life. According to Purkey, self-concept is not a cause of behavior, but acts as a relatively stable reference point for determining behavior. These major characteristics of self-concept have been supported by numerous researchers (Bracken et al., 2000; Byrne & Shavelson, 1987; Leonard, Beauvais, & Scholl, 1995; Marsh & Shavelson, 1985; Rosenberg, 1986).

Leonard et al., (1995) described the structure of the self-concept in four distinct areas. The nature of each component and its interaction with others results in a more complete definition of the self. These factors include: the perceived self, the ideal self, self-esteem, and social identities. The perceived self includes three attributes: traits, competencies, and values. Traits represent behaviors that are comparatively stable; they are behavior patterns that individuals repeat on a consistent basis. Competencies are ideas individuals have about the various talents, knowledge, skills, and abilities they possess. Values are guiding beliefs that are ranked by importance; and they assist in determining behavior based on the end result of participation in that behavior. The behaviors required to acquire the end result are compared to these values and a choice of whether to engage in those behaviors or not is made by the individual.

The second component of self-concept is the ideal self. The traits, competencies and values one wishes to have defines the ideal self. Self-esteem is the third component of self-concept, and it is used to tie the perceived self and ideal self together. Self-esteem is used to examine the self, and it may be defined as the difference between one's ideal self-perceptions and perceived self-perceptions. A person with little difference between ideal and perceived self will generally have high self-esteem. A person with a large difference between the ideal and perceived self will generally have low self-esteem (Leonard et al., 1995).

Social identities, the fourth component, are a reflection of an individual's self-concept; self-concept is used to designate the self in a social environment in a perceived category such as "teacher" or "student." Placement in a particular category is the result of past experience, learning, and current self-concept (Leonard et al., 1995). Based on these foundations, more recent approaches to studying self-concept examine it from a hierarchical perspective.

The Hierarchical Nature of Self-Concept

The hierarchical structure of self-concept may be defined by use of models. (Bracken et al., 2000; Bracken & Howell, 1991; Shavelson, Hubner, & Stanton, 1976). Marsh & Shavelson (1985) described the characteristics of these models of self-concept as follows:

1. It is multifaceted in that people categorize the vast amount of information they have about themselves and relate these categories to one another. The specific facets reflect the category system adopted by a particular individual and/or shared by a group.

2. It is hierarchically organized, with perceptions of behavior at the base moving to inferences about self in subareas (e.g., academic - English, science, history, mathematics), then to inferences about self in general.

3. General self-concept is stable, but as one descends the hierarchy, self-concept becomes increasingly situation specific and as a consequence less stable.

4. Self-concept becomes increasingly multifaceted as the individual moves from infancy to adulthood.

5. It has both a descriptive and an evaluative dimension such that individuals may describe themselves ("I am happy") and evaluate themselves ("I do well in mathematics").

6. It can be differentiated from other constructs such as academic achievement.

(p. 107)

As individuals age, especially from childhood through adolescence, more refined hierarchical components of self-concept become evident. An individual's self-concept moves from a generalized definition of self to a situational or context specific self-definition (e.g., from good student to good math student, average history student). The development of self-concept becomes increasingly based on the capacity to process abstract interpretations of the self. These interpretations of the self are products of an individual's passive and active existence in various environments (Bracken, 1992).

Environments have been defined as models of varying complexity, ranging from unidimensional models (general or global self-concept only) to multidimensional, hierarchical models (Bracken, 1992; Marsh & Hattie, 1996). Environments from the various multidimensional, hierarchical models have been arranged in several ways. Shavelson, Hubner, & Stanton (1976) described global, or general self-concept as being comprised of two main components: academic and non-academic self-concept. They posit academic self-concept could be further delineated into four distinct areas of self-concept: English, math, science, and history. Each of these areas could be further delineated until small 'parts' of self-concept were reached.

Other theorists (Bracken, 1992; Bracken et al., 2000; Byrne, 1984; Marx & Winne, 1980) have embraced the multidimensional, hierarchical depiction of self-concept, but have structured their models in different fashions. For example, Bracken proposed a seven-factor model, derived from six environmental contexts including family, social, academic, competence, physical, and affect self-concepts. These six components combine to form an individual's global or general self-concept. The six domains are not exclusive of one another, but have some commonalties. Bracken states, "This model presumes that the multiple dimensions that constitute self-concept are moderately intercorrelated. With domains overlapping to a moderate degree, it is presumed that at the center of all self-concept dimensions is a generalized self concept..." (p. 4).

The Development of Self-Concept

Self-perceptions are developed through exchange with one's surroundings. Feedback from the environment provides information that leads to the formation of attitudes, attitude change, and the creation of self-attributions. The two forms of information one receives are task and social feedback. The scrutiny of one's specific endeavors is task feedback. Social feedback is received from others in both a verbal and nonverbal manner. Social feedback results in direct and indirect attributions. Direct attributions refer to succinct communications, both verbal and written, regarding an individual's traits, competencies, or values. Indirect attributions are a result of informal means of feedback, and are often not meant as feedback by the communicator. "Body language," inclusion in social groups, and status level changes are examples of feedback that may lead to indirect attributions (Leonard et al., 1995).

The ideal self is developed through feedback from reference group members, and results in an individual being either inner-directed, or other-directed. Inner-directed individuals use favorable, unqualified feedback to internalize the traits, competencies, and values of the reference group. They develop their measure of ideal self from these internalized factors. Persons who are inner-directed use these internalized standards to determine their ideal self. They serve as their own "judge and jury" in determining whether they have attained their ideal self. Other-directed persons do not internalize the traits, competencies, or values of a social or reference group because of negative or provisional feedback. These individuals will seek feedback from the group on a consistent basis in order to compare their behaviors to those sanctioned by the reference group. In extreme cases, other-directed individuals may withdraw from a reference group, and attempt to find other external sources to measure the ideal self against.

Social identities are formed through the interaction of an individual with a social or reference group. As suggested above reference groups help an individual form the ideal self. Two social identities are usually constructed - a global identity, and a role specific identity. Global identity is that identity existing across most situations. It is the identity an individual wishes to indicate to others as their general self. A role specific identity exists for specific social situations and for specific groups of people.

Gender and Self-Concept

Modern perceptions regarding gender differences in adolescent self-concept are generally well founded. These perceptions hold that adolescent males have higher physical, affect, academic and competence self-concepts than females and that adolescent females have higher social and family self-concepts than males. There is no meaningful difference in global self-concept between males and females (Crain & Bracken, 1994; Jackson et al., 1994; Marsh, 1989; Marsh, 1993; Stake, 1992; Widamen et al., 1992; Wilgenbusch & Merrell, 1999). Wilgenbush and Merrell, in their meta-analysis of gender differences in self-concept, reported that those dimensions of self-concept having significant differences between males and females are relatively small in nature. Crain (1996) reported these differences as having little clinical significance. However, these authors warned that broad generalizations should not omit these small differences in self-concept between males and females. Therefore, the small differences that do exist between males and females in the domain areas of self-concept should be measured and evaluated.

Ethnicity and Self-Concept

Many studies examining ethnic and race differences in the self-concept of adolescents have been flawed for a variety of reasons, and they have yielded mixed findings (Aries, Olver, Blount, Christaldi, Fredman & Lee, 1998; Crain, 1996; Crain & Bracken, 1994; Widamen et al., 1992). Crain and Bracken (1994) reported significant differences of global self-concept scores of over 2000 African-American, Hispanic, and White adolescents between the ages of 10 and 18. They found African-American adolescents had significantly higher scores than their Hispanic or White counterparts. However, these authors noted the difference, though statistically significant, was less than one standard deviation from the mean self-concept scores of the sample. Aries et al. (1998) reported non-White subjects were significantly more aware of their race than were White subjects in their study of 78 students in the United States aged 18 to 23 years old. They suggested awareness of race in salient environments (e.g., public settings) may result in higher self-concept scores for White adolescents. In contrast, Widamen et al. (1992) reported that African-American adolescents had greater self-concepts than did Hispanic or White adolescents. They thought this occurred because of the reference group used by each group. African-American students were believed to use a lower standard to measure themselves against (e.g. African-American peers who generally scored low on achievement tests), resulting in greater scores on the self-concept measure. White and Hispanic adolescents, however, used a different standard (e.g., White adolescents, who generally scored high on achievement tests), resulting in lower scores on the self-concept measure.

Most conclusive findings regarding ethnic and racial differences in adolescent self-concept report little or no difference between groups. Crain and Bracken (1994) state, "Thus, both global and domain-specific self-concepts appear to be relatively impervious to differences among students' ethnic or cultural backgrounds" (p. 504). However, limitations to these studies such as lack of control for socioeconomic status may affect the above conclusion.

Change in Adolescent Self-Concept

Theorists argue that change in self-concept is a result of evaluation stemming from two sources — direct personal experience and interaction with others in a number of environments occurring over time (Bracken, 1992; Crain & Bracken, 1994). Adolescents "... learn specific and generalized response patterns both directly and indirectly through (a) their successes and failures in

14

various contexts, (b) the way others react to their actions, and (c) the manner in which others model behaviors and communicate expectations" (Crain & Bracken, p. 497). Adolescents are actors in numerous contexts or environments, and react to the stimuli in those contexts. Their actions, the results of these actions, and the results of past actions shape behavior over time (Bracken, 1992).

The adolescent evaluates actions in various contexts, and individual efficacy related to those actions. Four standards are used during this evaluation process: absolute (success or failure), ipsative (performance on a specific task compared to overall performance), comparative (performance likened to that of others), and ideal (expected performance) (Bracken, 1992). Thus, an individual in an environment receives feedback from him or herself as well as others, and uses these four standards to weigh that feedback. This evaluative process provides information to the individual that may affect one of (or any combination of) his or her domains of self-concept. Furthermore, as these evaluations and their associated behaviors become consistent over time, those behaviors come to represent the adolescent's self-concept related to that specific context or environment. Finally, the self-concepts from various contexts combine to form a general pattern of behavior, or a global self-concept (Bracken). Through the change in one or more domains of self-concept, an individual's general self-concept also changes.

Outdoor Adventure Education

Outdoor adventure education courses have been in existence since the early 1940s, when Kurt Hahn introduced Outward Bound (Hattie, Marsh, Neill & Richards, 1997). The original Outward Bound courses were designed to provide survival training to British sailors. The goals were to increase participants' independence, ability to rely on one self, and level of physical fitness. Over the past 40 years, outdoor adventure education programs have grown in both number and scope (Hattie et al., 1997). People participate in outdoor adventure education courses for a number of reasons, including learning new skills, creating new social contexts, experiencing the relationship of humans and nature, recreation, and increasing their self-confidence (Hazelworth & Wilson, 1990).

Outdoor adventure education courses are unique in that the participants are removed from their everyday environments. The inclusion of a physical activity, often where the level of risk is perceived by the participants to be greater than it actually is, constitutes a defining property of outdoor adventure education courses (Ewert, 1989). Although physical activity is often a major component of an outdoor adventure education course, physical fitness and physical skill development are not inclusively primary goals (Marsh, Richards, & Barnes, 1986).

Outdoor adventure education courses also require a group or individual to be self-reliant. Participants are responsible for carrying their own food, water, shelter, and clothing. They make decisions that directly affect their physical and emotional well-being. Most individuals and groups do not experience self-reliance in a foreign environment on a daily basis.

Outdoor adventure education courses are conducted in a variety of places. Backpacking, mountaineering, rock climbing, challenge (ropes) courses, paddling, hiking, and camping are commonly used to place individuals and groups in different circumstances than they are used to normally (Luckner, 1989). The combination of self-reliance, exposure to a different environment, and the experience of physical and mental challenges are used to meet the goals of outdoor adventure education courses (Marsh, Richards, & Barnes, 1986). These goals include increasing: self-concept, communication, confidence, problem-solving skills, attendance at school, academic performance, physical ability, reliance on others, and understanding of humans' role in the natural environment (Ewert, 1987; Gillett, Thomas, Skok, & McLaughlin, 1991; Hattie et al., 1997). Given the nature of these goals, outdoor adventure education courses have been offered to an ever-expanding group of participants. Today, business people, people with disabilities, youth at risk, senior citizens, school children, women's groups, support groups, individuals in recovery, professional sports teams, and college students regularly participate in such courses. However, much of the research that has been conducted has been focused on college students, adults, and 'special populations' (Hattie et al.; Finkenberg, Shows, & DiNucci, 1994).

Theories of Outdoor Adventure Education

Several theories have been developed to explain the outdoor adventure education phenomena. These theories include: optimal arousal, competence-effectance, self-efficacy, attribution, and competence/risk (Ewert, 1989; Priest, 1993).

Optimal arousal theory refers to the level of stimulation sought by an individual. It is influenced by the person's experience, and the environment in which the stimulation occurs. Generally, people will seek out levels of arousal that are consistent with their current level of skill and knowledge about their present situation. Factors contributing to arousal include: novelty, uncertainty, and complexity (Ewert, 1989). Experiences containing these factors incite the individual to learn new skills or knowledge to decrease the dissonance they encounter. This dissonance occurs when the individual's current level of expertise in an area is less than that required to successfully navigate an experience. This dissonance leads to a state of arousal, and to the learning of new skills and knowledge that may be applied to future situations. Outdoor adventure education courses create new situations in different environments for the participants. Ewert notes, "The uncertainty necessitates a change in behavior which generates knowledge about the success of the new behavior" (p. 88). Optimal arousal theory provides insight to how outdoor adventure education programs impact participants, although it does not fully explain all situations that arise.

Competence-effectance theory relates to an individual's need to exercise control over the environment. The human need for feeling capable and for self-determination in an environment leads people to find situations that are challenging and arousing (Ewert, 1989). The successful completion of these challenges leads to feelings of competence and finally, satisfaction. Competence-effectance theory may best be described by Csikszentmihalyi's Flow Model of Play (1975).

The Flow Model of Play suggests that as ability level increases, the level of challenge must also rise. When one's level of ability is congruent with the current challenge, feelings of 'flow' develop. Flow is characterized by loss of sense of time, focus becomes centered on the activity one is engaged in, and feelings of the "runner's high" or of "being in the zone" are encountered. A person with a high level of ability who faces an activity of low challenge experiences boredom, whereas a person with a low level of ability who faces an activity of high challenge experiences anxiety or worry. The Flow Model of Play suggests that individuals who participate in outdoor adventure education activities will strive to maximize their feelings of competence and self-determination. Through this process, characteristics of the self are changed through the experience of developing new skills to meet new or more difficult challenges (Csikszentmihalyi, 1975).

Self-efficacy theory (Bandura, 1977) has been recognized as one of the most influential theories in describing how outdoor adventure education affects participants (Ewert, 1989). Self-efficacy theory posits that individuals make estimates about their performance level in challenging or new situations. Individuals in outdoor adventure education activities are thus making judgments as to their performance level for a certain activity. Four processes of feedback exist once an individual has engaged in an activity. They are: 1) performance accomplishments, 2) vicarious experiences, 3) verbal persuasions, and 4) emotional arousal. Performance accomplishment is the actual engagement in an activity. It provides feedback that may be generalized and transferred to other situations. Vicarious experiences are those encounters where individuals can observe others' success or failure in an experience. The feedback from these observations affects an individual's beliefs about his or her performance in that activity. Verbal persuasion is depicted when a leader tells a participant she or he will be successful at an activity. Someone other than the participant has made an estimate of an individual's ability to complete that activity. Emotional arousal refers to feelings generated during participation in an activity. Performance accomplishments provide the most direct feedback to a participant that may be generalized to other situations (Ewert). Outdoor adventure education activities provide immediate feedback to the participant. Feelings of accomplishment are transferred to other situations and internalized, or attributed to oneself.

Attribution theory (Iso-Ahola, 1976) suggests individuals attempt to determine what causes an event, and then assign responsibility for the success or failure of that event to that cause. Attributions are either intrinsic/extrinsic and stable/unstable. The intrinsic/extrinsic nature of an attribution refers to where the motivation for participating in an activity comes from, either within the self (intrinsic) or outside the self (extrinsic). Stability refers to the likelihood an individual will participate in an activity in the future. Outdoor adventure education activities are most effective when participants' attributions are intrinsic and stable.

The performance accomplishment aspect of self-efficacy theory, when combined with attribution theory suggests that positive changes can occur to various facets of an individual's self-concept. The direct feedback of an outdoor adventure education activity allows participants to attribute their success to their ability to perform in that situation. This allows individuals to develop positive feelings about their ability to perform in new experiences.

Competence-risk theory (Priest, 1993) suggests that people use efficacy judgments and personal competencies to control the outcomes of participation in outdoor adventure education activities, conditional on their efficacy judgments being correct. "In short, they will be motivated to select risks which suit their level of perceived competence in the belief that they can positively influence the uncertainty of the adventure to a final outcome in their favor" (Priest, p. 50). Five outcomes result from the choice of the participant: 1) exploration and experimentation (low risk and high competence), 2) adventure (higher competence than risk, 3) peak adventure (congruent levels of competence and risk), 4) misadventure (higher risk than competence) and, 5) disaster (highest risk and lowest competency) (Priest). The competence-risk model suggests people will vary their involvement in outdoor activities based upon prior successes, intrinsic and extrinsic responses to their success or failures, and perceived self-efficacy beliefs for future challenges.

These are several of the theories that attempt to explain how and why people participate in outdoor adventure education activities. The common elements of these theories include expected outcomes in the form of efficacy beliefs and perceived levels of competence, activity levels congruent to perceived level of competence for maximum experience, and either positive or negative adjustments to perceived levels of competence and efficacy beliefs based on performance. Increased self-concept is often a result of participation in outdoor adventure education activities.

Change in Self-Concept as a Result of Outdoor Adventure Education

Outdoor adventure education activities contain many of the elements needed to affect self-concept included in Bracken's (1992) Environmental-Behavioral Interactive Model. Individuals participating in outdoor adventure education activities receive feedback through personal experience, through interaction with others, and are exposed to the successes and failures of other participants (Bandura, 1977; Priest, 1993). Bracken cites these as the three main ways in which adolescents' generalized response patterns are affected over time. As a result of these learned behaviors, he suggested self-concept is affected (1992).

Additionally, the manner in which this feedback is received through outdoor adventure education activities is much the same as the Environmental-Behavioral Interactive Model. The absolute evaluative standard (i.e., success or failure at an activity) of the Environmental-Behavioral Interactive Model mirrors the performance accomplishments feedback and evaluation component suggested in self-efficacy theory (Bandura, 1977), the intrinsic/extrinsic assignment of cause in attribution theory (Iso-Ahola, 1976), and the sufficient competence performed component of competence-risk theory (Priest, 1993).

The ipsative evaluative standard, or individual performance on a specific task compared to overall ability, of the Environmental-Behavioral Interactive Model may also be likened to the performance accomplishment component of self-efficacy theory. Further, ipsative evaluation may be compared to optimal arousal theory (Ewert, 1989). Optimal arousal theory posits the dissonance experienced through participation in one activity will cause an individual to generate knowledge about participating in new behaviors (Ewert), much the same as ipsative evaluation. Competence-effectance theory postulates individuals strive to maximize feelings of competence and self-determination. Through this process, characteristics of the self are changed through the experience of developing new skills to meet new or more difficult challenges (Csikszentmihalyi, 1975). Individuals using ipsative evaluation would thus compare their performance on an activity to their overall ability, and in the language of competence-effectance theory, become bored or anxious depending on their level of skill and the difficulty of the task. The Flow Model of Play (Csikszentmihalyi, 1975), and the increased/decreased competence component of the competence-risk model (Priest, 1993) represent ipsative evaluation.

An individual comparing his or her performance on an activity to the performance of others on that activity is using the comparative evaluation standard of Environmental-Behavioral Interactive Model. Outdoor adventure education activities provide ample opportunity to observe the success and failure of others, such as reaching the top of a rock climb or setting up a shelter that effectively sheds rain. The vicarious experience component of self-efficacy theory is the same as comparative evaluation.

Ideal, or expected, performance evaluation included in the Environmental-Behavioral Interactive Model is an inherent part of individual participation in outdoor adventure education activities. People participating in these experiences will set goals for their performance, often with the input of leaders and peers. Sometimes these goals will be attainable; other times they will be too great of a challenge and not be reached. The attainment of these goals and performance in activities in outdoor adventure activities will be evaluated using an ideal standard.

As suggested in the Environmental-Behavioral Interactive Model, the evaluation of behaviors in outdoor adventure education activities will become consistent over time. The consistency of these evaluations will be affected by internal and external feedback that has been evaluated using the four standards mentioned above. As these behaviors associated with outdoor adventure education activities become consistent, they will influence an individual's self-concept related to those behaviors. Additionally, self-concept related to other behaviors will be influenced as well. In essence, the behaviors associated with outdoor adventure education activities will be integrated into an individual's overall behavioral pattern. This integration will first occur in the domains of self-concept, which in turn will be integrated into an individual's general behavior pattern and thus affect general, or global self-concept (Bracken, 1992).

Outdoor Adventure Education and Self-Concept: Previous Studies

Changes in self-concept resulting from participation in outdoor adventure education courses have been the topic of many studies. However, the populations studied, the methods used, and the results obtained have varied. An early study by Kaplan (1974) examined the psychological benefits of outdoor challenge programs. She examined the impact that a two-week outdoor program had on 10 males aged 15 to 17 years. Kaplan used a control group of 25 people matched to those subjects participating in the program for area of residence and age. Scores from the Rosenberg Self-Esteem measure were compared using a t-test, with findings indicating a significantly higher score for those participating in the outdoor challenge program. However, the small sample size and use of a global measure of self-esteem limit the generalizability and implications of this study, as does the inclusion of only male participants. Kaplan indicated the lack of theoretical underpinnings regarding self-esteem and self-concept at the time and the limited scope of the programs were flaws in her study. Although there are theoretical and statistical faults to her study, it laid the foundation for research in this area.

Lambert et al. (1978) studied changes in self-concept and self-actualization in college students who took part in a 30-day academic class with an outdoor adventure component lasting one week. They used an experimental form of the Tennessee Self-Concept Scale to measure the self-concept of 104 participants, including 57 males and 47 females. The Tennessee Self-Concept Scale included 10 subscales, each measuring a domain of total self-concept, which was an improvement in theoretical design over previous studies. Additionally, Lambert and his colleagues utilized three control groups resulting in an improved research design as well. However, the authors reported the most significant and reliable score on the Tennessee Self-Concept Scale was that for total self-concept. They reported significant findings for five of the ten domains as well as for Total Self-Concept for the experimental group. However, Lambert et al. noted that those students participating in the class with the outdoor adventure component registered specifically for that course and indicated this as a possible sign of greater initial levels of self-concept that could possibly skew the results. The non-random assignment of participants to the control groups was also cited as a limitation of this study.

Marsh and his colleagues (1986) were among the first to use a theoretically sound model of self-concept while studying the effects of participating in traditional Outward Bound programs (e.g., 26-day "Standard Courses"). These researchers used the Self-Description Questionnaire, which is based on a multidimensional, hierarchical model of self-concept (i.e., Shavelson et al., 1976) to collect data on over 350 participants. However, three-quarters of the subjects were men providing an unequal balance in data for females. Marsh et al. took several measurements of self-concept and utilized analysis of variance and t-tests providing a sound statistical method for analyzing the data. They reported significant findings for all domains of self-concept, and recognized different magnitudes of change for these domains indicating programmatic impacts could affect specific domains of self-concept without affecting others. The primary flaw with this study was the lack of a control group for comparative purposes. These researchers did not attempt to control for any preexisting differences in self-concept, using separate measures as a means of comparing changes in magnitude of self-concept only.

Marsh and Richards (1988) examined low-achieving high school students who also participated in an Outward Bound program called the Bridging Course. This program used a six-week residential setting focusing on individualized learning and included some physical components of Outward Bound standard courses. Sixty-six male Australian public high school students participated in the study. These authors used a multiple time series design with five different groups over a four-year time period. However, no comparison group was used, somewhat weakening this study. Additionally, no female participants were used restricting the generalizability of the findings. Most participants also reported their family socioeconomic status as lower and lower-middle class and as migrants, further limiting the generalizability of the findings. However, Marsh and Richards reported significant results in academic self-concept as measured by the Self-Description Questionnaire as an outcome of participation in the Outward Bound Bridging Course. These authors reported incremental increases between each of the measurement periods as well, indicating short-term gains in specific areas of self-concept may occur in an adolescent population. Marsh and Richards also affirmed the multidimensional nature of self-concept.

Luckner (1989) studied the effects of participating in a ten-day winter outdoor adventure course on the self-concept of people with hearing impairments. Twenty people (16 females and 4 males) took part in this program, which does not allow for adequate statistical power. However, this researcher utilized a quasi-experimental design by including a control group in the analysis. A multiple time series design was used with measurements of self-concept occurring upon arrival at the program, after ten days, and at two-month follow-up date. An analysis of covariance design was used to examine the data, using the first measure of self-concept as the covariate. This process adjusted for initial discrepancies in self-concept between participants. Luckner reported significantly increased self-concept in the experimental group at both the ten day and two month follow-up measurements. The results indicate the effectiveness of an outdoor adventure education course in increasing self-concept of people with hearing-impairments. However, the small sample size dramatically impacts the findings of this study.

Hazelworth and Wilson (1990) conducted a study with teenagers participating in a nine-day adventure camp program. They used the Tennessee Self-Concept Scale to record pretest and posttest self-concept scores of thirty-nine subjects. Using a t-test to analyze their data, Hazelworth and Wilson reported significant findings for only nine of forty-five items measured. This may be attributed to low statistical power due to the small sample size used. Also, the significant changes occurred in only four of nine domains of self-concept as measured by the Tennessee Self-Concept Scale. The authors note the lack of a control group as a limitation to this study as well. The small sample size and marginal results of this study lend little credibility to gains in self-concept as a result of participating in an adventure camp program.

A study conducted in 1991 by Gillett et al. provides strong support for gains in self-concept from participating in short-term outdoor adventure education courses. These authors used the Tennessee Self-Concept Scale and the Coopersmith Self-Esteem Inventory in a pretest-posttest format to measure changes in self-concept as a result of participating in a six-day experience. An experimental group of twenty-seven males and thirty-four females (sixty-one total) was compared to a control group of sixteen (twelve males and four females) for a total sample of seventy-six using a t-test. Gillett et al. indicated that the homogeneity of variance was tenable for the analyses, lending to the strength of the findings. They reported significant gains in two of nine domains of self-concept, as well as in total self-concept as measured by the Tennessee Self-Concept Scale for the experimental group. There were none for the control group. Gillett et al. reported significant differences on the Coopersmith Self-Esteem Inventory as well. The use of a larger sample size and sound statistical analyses provide support for the authors' contention that short-term outdoor programs affect self-concept.

Finkenberg et al. (1994) considered participation in adventure-based activities and the self-concept of college students. A quasi-experimental design was used to compare an experimental group comprised of eight women and ten men to a control group of seventeen women and fifteen men. However, only individuals of the same gender were compared (i.e., men to men, women to women). The small sample size does not allow for statistical power. An analysis of covariance was used to analyze pretest and posttest differences on the Tennessee Self-Concept Scale, using the pretest scores as the covariate. Significant differences between the control and experimental group for men were found on three of nine domain scores as well as on the total score. For women, significant differences existed on two of nine domain scores as well as the total score. The findings of this study are questionable due to the small sample size and the lack of comparison of the total experimental group to the total control group. However, the differences that were found do support changes in self-concept in college students from participation in adventure-based activities.

Cason and Gillis (1994), in their meta-analysis of outdoor adventure programming for adolescents, provide evidence as to the success of increasing adolescent self-concept. They report an effect size of $d = .34$ for over sixty studies related to adolescent self-concept and participation in outdoor adventure programs. These authors do not, however, distinguish an effect size for typical adolescents participating in these programs. Cason and Gillis found longer programs and younger participants were linked to greater effect sizes. They also found that quasi-experimental and experimental studies reported lower effect sizes than survey or single group research. Finally, Cason

23

and Gillis reported higher effect sizes were found in published studies and lower effect sizes appeared in unpublished dissertations.

A meta-analysis by Hattie et al. (1997), reported findings of effect sizes (Cohen's d) ranging from .11 to .51 for changes in various domains of adolescent self-concept as a result of participating in outdoor adventure programs. Reported effect sizes include: .38 for overall self-concept in follow-up studies, physical ability: .50, peer relations: .32, general: .49, physical appearance: .47, academic: .43, confidence: .32, self-efficacy: .51, family: .24, self-understanding: .24, and well-being: .11. Hattie et al. reported no differences between males and females. Additionally, their analyses confirmed that programs of longer duration have a greater effect on changes in self-concept. This study provides overwhelming support for changes in adolescent self-concept, and appears to be well grounded in both theoretical application and statistical technique.

There are several factors that are evident weaknesses in the existing literature regarding outdoor adventure education and adolescent self-concept. Sample sizes used in previous studies often were not large enough to allow for appropriate statistical power. Further, the lack of control or comparison groups in several studies is a limitation. Additionally, many studies used simple statistical tests (e.g., a t-test) to compare group means when other tests such as an analysis of variance should have been used.

A second area of weakness among existing studies is the lack of use of covariates that may affect self-concept (Neill, 1997). Existing research assumes changes in self-concept are a sole result of participation in the outdoor adventure education program. Effects of everyday life experiences are not considered. Further, repeated measures techniques were not used in many studies. The current literature is generally based on pretest - posttest measures of self-concept.

The generalizability of existing studies is limited as well. There is limited research on outdoor adventure education experiences of short duration or consisting of several short experiences. Neill (1997) states, "As pressure is applied to outdoor educators to deliver shorter and shorter programs, it is important that the implications of program length suggested by the research findings are taken into account" (p. 5). Additionally, currently existing studies often used Outward Bound participants as participants, limiting the generalizability of the findings to other populations. Female participants were underrepresented in existing studies, possibly affecting the findings and their generalizability.

Although there have been many studies examining outdoor adventure education programs and adolescent self-concept, these studies do not provide a full picture as to how individuals' self-concepts are affected. The demand for shorter programs and lack of research on these types of programs, need for sound statistical methods in research related to adolescent self-concept and outdoor adventure education, and limited research on programs not using Outward Bound participants as subjects were evident in the current literature.

CHAPTER III

THE METHOD

As indicated in the literature review, many studies examining adolescent self-concept and outdoor adventure education were flawed because they were based on dated theoretical models of self-concept, had limited statistical power due to small sample sizes, used faulty statistical techniques, provided no control or comparison groups, or ignored independent variables affecting the participants' self-concept. Furthermore, typical adolescent populations have not been extensively used as subjects, especially in short-term, academically based programs. To such, this investigator proposed to examine the changes in self-concept of typical students enrolled in a traditional college-preparatory high school. A contemporary, hierarchical model of self-concept was used, a statistically and theoretically proven measurement instrument based upon this model was utilized, and appropriate statistical techniques for a quasi-experimental research design were employed to analyze the data. Additionally, upon the suggestion of previous researchers (Cason and Gillis, 1994; Hattie et al., 1997), covariates were included to control for some inherent differences among and between subjects. The effects of variables such as previous outdoor experience, perceived risk associated with outdoor activities, and current risk taking behaviors were examined. The New York University Committee on Activities Involving Human Subjects approved the protocol for the collection of data in this study.

Site and Population

A convenience sample of ninth, tenth, eleventh, and twelfth grade students was used as a source for participants in this study. They were recruited from Friends Seminary, a private school in New York City, New York. Friends Seminary educates students from kindergarten through twelfth grade, under the care of the New York Quarterly Meeting of Religious Society of Friends. Education occurs within the context of Quaker beliefs. The upper school had a total of 233 students during the Fall 2000 semester.

The Experiential Education Department at Friends Seminary offers a series of required and elective courses to the high school student population. Tenth grade students are required to take a one semester outdoor adventure education course entitled "Experiential Education." Eleventh and twelfth grade students may take an elective course entitled "Wilderness." Both the Experiential Education and Wilderness courses include classroom instruction, practical experience, and at least two outdoor adventure overnight experiences.

Previous meta-analyses reported effect sizes of d = .34 (Cason and Gillis, 1994) and d = .38 (Hattie et al., 1997) for outdoor adventure education programs and changes in adolescent self-concept. This study used the average of these effect sizes (d = .36) in determining an adequate sample size to ensure appropriate statistical power. Cohen (1988) indicates statistical power of at least .80 should be used. The 94 participants exceeded the number (64) needed for the effect size.

Groups

Two groups of subjects were compared. The experimental group consisted of 36 ninth, tenth, eleventh and twelfth grade students (25 males, 11 females) enrolled in the Fall 2000 semester Experiential Education and Wilderness courses. The comparison group consisted of 58 ninth, tenth, eleventh and twelfth grade students (20 males, 38 females) not enrolled in the Fall 2000 Experiential Education or Wilderness courses. Random assignment to these groups was not possible. However, for the tenth grade students who were required to take the Experiential Education course, there was no systematic method used to designate in which semester they took the course. Enrollment in the course was based only upon broad scheduling factors (e.g., conflicts with required courses). The eleventh and twelfth grade students who enrolled in the Wilderness course choose to do so during the Fall Semester, resulting in no systematic enrollment of students in the Wilderness course. Since random assignment was not possible, there was no assurance that males and females would be equally represented in the experimental and comparison groups. However, based on past class compositions, approximately equal numbers of males and females were expected to be in each class at the beginning of the semester (M.C. Breunig, personal communication, January 21, 2000).

Program Description

The Experiential Education class met two times a week for 40 minutes per period during the Fall 2000 semester. Classroom instruction included skills training for camping/backpacking and rock climbing, and philosophical and theoretical information regarding outdoor adventure education and experiential education. Skills training was comprised of: minimum impact camping techniques (i.e., how to leave no trace when using a natural area); belaying and knots for rock climbing; dressing for and being outdoors in various weather conditions; how to pack a backpack; setting up shelters; health and basic first aid; and backcountry hygiene and camp sanitation. Students viewed videotapes presenting information on preventing hypothermia and procedures to follow for minimum impact camping.

Theoretical and philosophical information tracing the history and development of outdoor adventure education and experiential education was presented through class lecture and reading assignments. Groups of two or three students gave a short (i.e., ten to fifteen minute) presentation on a subject of their choice related to outdoor adventure education in class. The students participated in a three-day, two-night rock climbing trip, as well as a three-day, two night backpacking trip. Each student assigned him or herself a midterm grade based on self-assessment of the application of outdoor skills and knowledge. The instructors based on a 21-point scale testing skills and knowledge application assigned final grades.

The Wilderness class met two times a week for 40 minutes per period during the Fall 2000 semester as well. Wilderness students were provided skills training related to sea kayaking, backcountry skiing, and winter camping. Theoretical and philosophical information related to wilderness history, sea kayaking technique, and ethics of backcountry travel was presented through class lecture and reading assignments. Students reviewed how to tie knots commonly used in camping situations (e.g., taut line hitch, bowline, trucker's hitch), setting up shelters (tents and tarps), and dressing for and being in various weather conditions. Additionally, students received skills instruction in stove lighting, menu planning, winter camping, and backcountry skiing. Theoretical and philosophical information regarding wilderness history was provided through class lecture. Students were asked to read several articles written by prominent nature writers, as well as write their own nature essays. Students in the wilderness class participated in a four-day, three-night sea kayaking trip in Maryland, as well as a four-day, three-night backcountry skiing trip in Vermont. The instructors assigned students grades.

Program Faculty

These same instructors taught the classroom and outdoor components of both the Experiential Education and Wilderness courses. One instructor is male, the other female. The male instructor had 15 years experience leading outdoor adventure education activities, had advanced wilderness first-aid training, was a qualified sea kayak and backcountry ski instructor, and had worked at Friends Seminary for 12 years. The female instructor had 12 years experience leading outdoor adventure education activities, had advanced wilderness first-aid training, was a licensed New York State Tier II Rock Climbing Guide, and had a Master of Arts degree in Experiential Education. Additionally, these instructors had worked together teaching and leading the Experiential Education and Wilderness courses and outdoor adventure education activities for five years previous to the Fall 2000 semester. Further, both instructors were members of the Association for

29

Experiential Education, a nonprofit organization for outdoor adventure education professions. The inclusion of one female and one male provided a balanced leadership team in terms of gender.

Instrumentation

The Multidimensional Self-Concept Scale (Bracken, 1992) the Life Events Survey (Lewis, Siegel, & Lewis, 1984), and a short demographic questionnaire were used for this study.

Multidimensional Self-Concept Scale

The Multidimensional Self Concept Scale (MSCS; Bracken, 1992) was used as the measure of adolescent self-concept for this study. The MSCS is a 150-item scale based on the multidimensional, hierarchical model of self-concept proposed by Shavelson, Hubner, and Stanton (1976), and is solidly grounded in contemporary self-concept theory (Byrne, 1996). This instrument contains six subscales of 25 questions each: social self-concept (sample question, "Most people like me"), competence self-concept (sample question, "I am very self confident"), affect self-concept (sample question, "I have good self control"), academic self-concept (sample question, "I usually do well on tests"), family self-concept (sample question, "My family is no good"), and physical self-concept (sample question, "I feel good about how I look"). A global self-concept score is obtained by using all 150 questions. The MSCS assumes the modest intercorrelation of these domains of self-concept as well as with the general, or global self-concept (Byrne).

The MSCS was designed for use with children and adolescents in grades five through twelve, and may be administered in a group or individual setting (Bracken, 1992). It was written for a third grade reading level, and is of self-report format. Items were worded in a simple fashion and do not include slang or colloquialisms enabling the MSCS to be used in urban, rural and suburban settings in the United States. Additionally, this assists in reducing bias due to gender or ethnicity (Byrne, 1996). Questions were worded positively and negatively in order to avoid response bias. Subjects responded to questions using a 4-point Likert scale which confronts possible central tendency response-set bias. The six domain self-concept scores (from the subscales) were produced through the summation of items relating to that domain after recoding negatively worded questions (minimum score of 25, maximum score of 100) for each scale. A general self-concept score was produced through the summation of all items after recoding those questions that were negatively worded (minimum score of 150, maximum score of 600).

Psychometrically, the MSCS is a sound instrument (Archambault, 1995; Bracken, 1992; Bracken & Howell, 1991; Bracken & Mills, 1994; Byrne, 1996; Rotatori, 1994; Willis, 1995). The

MSCS was normed on a sample of 2,501 children aged 9 to 19 years old. Data were collected from seventeen sites around the United States, which bodes well for the general use of this instrument (Byrne). However, some reviewers noted that the Northeastern region of the United States was underrepresented and the South over represented in this sample, possibly weakening its validity for use in the entire United States (Rotatori; Willis). However, when compared to other popular measures of self-concept such as the Self-Description Questionnaire, Self-Perception Profile for Children, the Tennessee Self-Concept Scale, and the Piers-Harris Children's Self-concept Scale, the MSCS was standardized on a larger and more geographically diverse sample (Archambault; Bracken).

The MSCS has acceptable internal consistency alphas of .98 for the total scale, and .87 to .97 for the subscales (Bracken, 1992; Byrne, 1996). Internal consistency alphas by grade level are also acceptable: .97 to .99 per grade for the total scale, and .85 to .97 per grade for the subscales (Bracken). Test-retest reliability is acceptable as well (i.e., .90 for the entire scale and .73 to .81 for the subscales). The MSCS was tested for significant differences over time using a Bonferroni correction of t-test results with no significant differences being revealed (Byrne). However, these findings were based on a sample of 37 subjects for a 4-week interval providing limited evidence for this claim (Archambault, 1995).

The concurrent validity of the instrument is proven through correlations with the Coopersmith Self-Esteem Inventory Total Scale (correlations ranging from .57 to .73), with the Piers-Harris Children's Self-Concept Scale subscales (correlations ranging from .66 to .77), and with the Self-Descriptive Questionnaires I & II (correlations for the total scales were .69 and .80 respectively) (Archambault, 1995; Rotatori, 1994).

A five instrument factor analysis was conducted for construct validity (Bracken, 1992). The MSCS, Coopersmith Self-Esteem Inventory, Piers-Harris Children's Self-Concept Scale, Self-Esteem Index, and Tennessee Self-Concept Scale were analyzed. The results supported the total self-concept factor as well as the six subscales. The Competence subscale, however, was not recommended for independent interpretation, as proportion of specific variance is low, proportion of common variance is high, and internal consistency is low when compared to the other five subscales (Bracken; Willis, 1995).

The MSCS was also tested for construct validity by using it to compare students previously identified with low self-concepts to typical students. The MSCS was found to distinguish between these two groups (Byrne, 1996). The construct validity was again established through confirming the ability of the MSCS to discriminate respective constructs on other scales (e.g., the Assessment of Interpersonal Relations Scale). The MSCS has been proven to be an acceptable instrument to use to measure self-concept.

Life Events Survey

A measure of experiences was included as a means of determining if there were any major occurrences (e.g., death of a parent, moving to a new residence) that may affect an adolescent's self-concept. The Life Events Survey (Lewis, Siegel & Lewis, 1984) is a 20-item measure, designed for use with adolescents, that examines stress-provoking circumstances related to major life events as well as everyday occurrences (sample question, "Not having homework done on time"). Participants were asked to specify whether or not an experience has occurred within a specific time frame and to rate those experiences that did occur using a five-point Likert scale (1 - "not bad," 2 - "a little bad," 3 - "pretty bad," 4 - "real bad," and 5 - "terrible" (Brown & Siegel, 1988; Lewis et al., 1984). A stress score was produced by adding the rating scores reported by the participant for those events that occurred with a possible range of 0 to 100. (Lewis et al.).

The Life Events Survey was originally normed using a sample of 2,480 students, of approximately equal numbers of males and females, and included various racial and ethnic groups (Lewis et al., 1984). Participants were selected from communities of varying size and socioeconomic status in different areas of the United States. This instrument showed an internal consistency level of .82 (Lewis et al.). A factor analysis was conducted producing three components: sources of anxiety, sources of depression, and living arrangements (Lewis et al.). The authors reported that females generally rate items as being worse more than males, and found ethnic/racial differences in responses as well. However, females and males ranked the items in the scale in a similar manner as to how "bad" each item was perceived (Lewis et al.).

Scores from the Life Events Survey were utilized by the investigator to determine if any of the participants experienced events that would artificially affect their self-concept. Students scoring more than four standard deviations higher than the group mean were eliminated from subsequent analyses.

Demographic Survey

A short demographic questionnaire was also administered. Data regarding each student's gender, age, ethnicity, grade in school, and academic performance were collected. Additionally, eleven items asking the student to report his or her perceived level of outdoor skill, perception of risk associated with outdoor adventure education activities, and personal risk taking behaviors was included in the demographic survey. Responses to these items were recorded on a five point Likert scale ranging from 0 to 4. The first three items were combined to form a perceived risk score (range 0 to 12), the next three items formed a risk taking behavior score (range 0 to 12), and the final four items formed an outdoor experience score (range 0 to 16). Face validity for this instrument has been established through its use in previous studies relating to outdoor adventure education activities (Young & Ewert, 1992). However, reliability and validity have not been extensively tested (A. Young, personal communication, May 2, 2000).

Setting

The instrument was administered during three prearranged class meetings in which students from each grade level are assembled. For each measurement session, the students met in an assigned room in the Friends Seminary school building, New York City. Each student had a place to sit by him or herself. The researcher was present to ensure conditions remained as constant as possible for each participant at the beginning of each session. Accommodations for proper lighting and temperature control were made with the school administration. The investigator supplied pencils for all respondents. School personnel maintained a quiet atmosphere conducive to answering the instruments.

Procedures

This investigator used the following procedures.

Instrument Administration

The MSCS, Life Events Survey and demographic form were administered to the participants three times during the Fall 2000 semester. The first data collection occurred during the second week of classes. The second data collection occurred one week before the students in the outdoor adventure education courses commenced the outdoor experience component of the course. The third data collection occurred the third week of December 2000. Students were allotted 45 minutes to complete the survey at each session.

Recruitment and Informed Consent

During the first week of school during the Fall 2000 semester, students eligible to participate in this study were gathered by the school administration in a common meeting place at Friends Seminary, New York City. The researcher was present at this meeting to explain the purpose and procedures of the study and to ask for volunteers. Any student in the Upper School at Friends Seminary was eligible to participate. Specifically, the researcher said, "My name is Tim O'Connell. I am a doctoral student in the Department of Health Studies at New York University. I am asking students to volunteer to participate in a study to learn more about the effects of participating in various courses at Friends Seminary and adolescent development. If you choose to volunteer, you will be asked to fill out a questionnaire at 3 separate times during the Fall 2000 Semester. It will take about 40 minutes to complete the questionnaire each time - this will be done at a scheduled time in school. Your participation is completely voluntary. You may end your involvement at any point. Only group information will be reported; your name will never be connected with your responses. Only the study's overall results will be shared with Friends Seminary. If you are interested in volunteering, please take an information packet home to your parent or guardian. If you choose to participate, or choose not to participate in this study, your grades, academic standing or ability to receive services at Friends Seminary will not be affected. I will be in school tomorrow morning to collect the forms signed by your parent or guardian."

After explaining the aims and methods for the study and answering any questions, the researcher gave any interested student a cover letter from the Upper School Headmaster, a letter explaining the study, and two copies of the informed consent form for the student to take home to his or her parents/guardians. Informed consent was obtained from each student's parent or guardian prior to his or her participation in the study following procedures as outlined by the New York University Committee on Activities Involving Human Subjects. Informed consent was obtained from those students whose parents gave permission to participate in the study during the first data collection session. These students were given a signed copy to keep. After the researcher provided the students with an opportunity to read the informed consent form, he answered their various questions. No data were collected from any student until signed informed consent forms were obtained from both the parent/guardian and the student.

Data Collection Procedures

Each data collection session followed the same procedures. Students were gathered in an assigned meeting place. The researcher took general attendance in order to be able to collect data at a later time from absent subjects, as well as to excuse those students who did not have informed consent from their parents/guardians. Those who did not have informed consent were excused to another room where school personnel supervised them. Students were given a pencil, the demographic questionnaire, the Multidimensional Self-Concept Scale, and the Life Events Survey.

The instruments were distributed as a packet with a confidential code number that had been individually assigned to each participant prior to the first data collection session by the investigator. The researcher explained the purpose of the study to the students, reminded them that their participation was voluntary, and that they may stop at any time during the session.

Then, the researcher said, "Do not mark anything on your answer sheet until specifically asked to do so." The researcher then read aloud the directions for the Multidimensional Self-Concept Scale. Specifically, the researcher said, "Please rate the following statements according to how well the statement applies to you. There are no right or wrong answers, but it is important that you rate each statement according to how you honestly feel. Be sure to be honest with yourself as you consider the statement you are rating. To mark your answer, simply circle the letters that correspond with your feelings toward the statement. Each statement should be rated as: Strongly Agree (SA), Agree (A), Disagree (D), Strongly Disagree (SD). You may stop filling out the questionnaire at any point, and do not have to answer any questions you do not want to answer. Does anyone have any questions?" The researcher did not read any portion of the questionnaire to the students, except for the directions for each of the three sections.

After answering any questions, the researcher said, "Please turn to page eight of your answer sheet. For this section, the directions are as follows: The following is a list of things that some teens say make them feel bad or nervous or make them worry. Please mark "yes" if that happened to you in the past year, or "no" if it did not happen to you in the past year ("Past year" was only be used on the first measurement. For the second and third measurement, the directions were amended to reflect the period of time between measurements). If it did happen to you, please indicate how you felt about it by placing an "X" next to "not bad," "a little bad," "pretty bad," "real bad," or "terrible." You do not have to answer any questions you do not want to answer. Does anyone have any questions regarding this section?"

After answering any questions, the researcher said, "Please turn to page ten of your answer sheet. Please fill in answers for questions 1 to 8 as best as possible. For question 9, the directions are as follows. Listed below are a number of contrasting statements. Some refer to outdoor activities such as rock climbing, backpacking, sea kayaking or camping; other refer to you. Please circle the number that best represents your feelings or perceptions. There are no right or wrong answers. You do not have to answer any questions you do not want to answer. Does anyone have any questions?" After answering any questions, the researcher said, "Please begin." The researcher left the room at this point. Students were allocated up to 45 minutes for each data collection session. Upon completion, each student submitted the survey packet to the researcher who was directly outside the room and returned to his or her seat. Data was collected from absent students who were willing to participate and had their parents'/guardians' signed informed consent form as soon as possible using the procedures above.

<u>Confidentiality</u>

The researcher assigned each participant a code number to be used to track each participant's responses over the course of the three data collection sessions. Only the researcher kept the list of names and code numbers; no one from Friends Seminary had access to this list. The list of names and code numbers were kept in a locked file cabinet in the researcher's home. Only code numbers were used to identify data. Completed questionnaires were immediately collected by the researcher and kept in a locked file cabinet in the researcher's home. No one from Friends Seminary had access to the completed questionnaires. Findings were reported only in aggregate form. Completed questionnaires and informed consent forms will be destroyed three years after completion of the study. After data collection and data entry were completed, the researcher destroyed the list of names and code numbers of students.

<u>Data Analysis</u>

Scores on each of the instruments were produced as suggested by the corresponding instruction manual. The data were entered and was analyzed using the commercially available Statistical Package for the Social Sciences (SPSS, Version 10). Means, standard deviations, numbers in each group, and correlation tables for all variables were obtained for the entire sample, the experimental and comparison groups, and males and females. Histograms and bar charts were produced as appropriate to the data for each of the major variables. Demographic data were calculated for the entire sample, experimental and comparison groups, and males and females. Total scores on the Life Events Survey were calculated and reviewed. Any student scoring four or more standard deviations higher than the mean of the total group score on either the MSCS or Life Events Survey was deemed an outlier and was not used in subsequent analyses. Reliability analysis was conducted on each of the major instruments.

Hypotheses one through nine were examined using a repeated measures analysis of covariance (ANCOVA). The ANCOVA was used to examine the difference in general self-concept scores and each of the six domain self-concept scores between the experimental and comparison groups (hypotheses one through seven), and between males and females in the experimental group (hypotheses eight and nine). The total scores from the perceived risk, personal outdoor experience, and risk taking behavior scales and corresponding MSCS score from the baseline data were evaluated as covariates, and used as appropriate.

Diagnostic tests to meet assumptions such as homogeneity of variance were conducted as part of each repeated measure ANCOVA analysis. Finally, the ANCOVA was implemented using an alpha level of .05 or less for significance.

CHAPTER IV

THE RESULTS

The purpose of this study was to examine the effects of participating in a one semester-long adventure education course on the self-concept of high school students. Because previous researchers have suggested change is most apt to take place in the domains of self-concept, these domains (affect, social, physical, family, competence, and academic) as well as general self-concept were examined (Crain & Bracken, 1994; Jackson, Hodge, & Ingram, 1994; Marsh, 1993; Rosenberg, 1986; Widamen et al., 1992). Self-reported risk taking behaviors, personal outdoor experience, perceived risk of outdoor adventure activities, and corresponding Multidimensional Self Concept Scale (MSCS) scores (domain or global) from the baseline data were used as covariates, as appropriate. A repeated measures analysis of covariance (ANCOVA) was used to determine if there were any significant differences in general self-concept and each of the domains of self-concept between students taking either of two semester-long outdoor adventure education courses and students not taking either of these courses.

Additionally, a repeated measures ANCOVA was used to determine if there were significant differences in general self-concept and each of the domains of self-concept between males and females enrolled in the outdoor adventure education courses. Demographic and descriptive statistics are reported. Then the results are presented related to the stated hypotheses.

Data Collection

Data were collected at three points in time during the Fall 2000 semester. One hundred high school students of 233 (or 42.9%) enrolled at Friends Seminary returned signed parent informed consent forms. Baseline data were collected during the first week of classes on September 13, 2000. Of the 100 students who indicated interest in participating in this study, 95 completed the student informed consent form, MSCS, demographic questionnaire (which included self-reported perceived risk taking behaviors, previous outdoor experience, and perceived risk of outdoor activities), and the Life Events Survey.

The second data collection occurred on October 18, 2000, which directly preceded the start of the outdoor trip component of the adventure education courses. Ninety-four students of the original 95 (98.9%) who participated in the baseline data collection took part in the second wave. The third and final wave occurred during the final week of the semester on December 13, 2000. This was directly after the completion of the outdoor trip component of the adventure education

39

courses. Ninety-four participants took part in the third wave, resulting in a final sample of 40.3% of high school students at Friends Seminary.

Demographic Characteristics

Demographic and descriptive statistics were determined for the sample of 94 students using the Statistical Package for Social Sciences (SPSS) version 10.0. For the total sample, the mean age reported by participants was 15.18 years (SD = 1.00), with a range from 13 to 18. Students taking outdoor adventure education courses reported a mean age of 15.31 years (SD = .71), and students not taking outdoor adventure education courses reported a mean age of 15.10 (SD = 1.15). See Table 1 for frequencies and percents for these groups as well as the total sample.

Table 1

Age of Respondents for Total Sample and by Enrollment in Outdoor Adventure Education Courses

Age	Total		Taking Outdoor Adventure Education		Not Taking Outdoor Adventure Education	
	n	$\%$	n	$\%$	n	$\%$
13	1	1.1	0	0	1	1.7
14	25	26.6	2	5.6	23	39.7
15	35	37.2	24	66.7	11	19.0
16	23	24.5	7	19.4	16	27.6
17	9	9.6	3	8.3	6	10.3
18	1	1.1	0	0	1	1.7

There were approximately an equal number of males and females, with 47.9% (n = 45) being male and 52.1% (n = 49) being female. Figure 1 indicates the total number of males and females who participated in this study, as well the number of those males (n = 25) and females (n = 11) who were enrolled in outdoor adventure education courses.

40

Figure 1

Males and Females in Total Sample and Taking Outdoor Adventure Education Courses

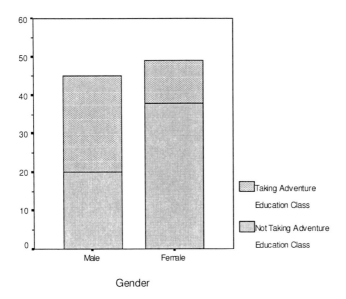

Gender

When asked about the number of outdoor trips they had taken in the previous two years, student responses ranged from no trips to 20 trips ($\underline{M}$ = 2.85, $\underline{SD}$ = 3.02) for the total sample. Students taking outdoor adventured education courses reported taking a range of no trips to 10 trips ($\underline{M}$ = 2.61, $\underline{SD}$ = 2.16). Outdoor trips taken by students not enrolled in the outdoor adventure education courses ranged from no trips to 20 trips ($\underline{M}$ = 3.00, $\underline{SD}$ = 3.45).

A majority of the students (71.3%) indicated their ethnicity as European/Caucasian/White (n = 67). Of the remaining 28.7%, students reported their ethnicity as follows: 9 (9.6%) were African American/Black, 9 (9.6%) were of mixed race, 7 (7.4%) indicated being Latino/Latina/Hispanic, and 2 (2.1%) were Asian or Pacific Islander. Of the 36 students enrolled in outdoor adventure education courses, 3 (8.3%) were African American/Black, 26 (72.2%) were European/Caucasian/White, 5 (13.9%) were Latino/Latina/Hispanic, and 2 (5.6%) were of mixed race. Students not enrolled in outdoor adventure education courses ($\underline{n}$ = 58) reported their ethnicity as follows: 6 (10.3%) were African American/Black, 2 (3.4%) were Asian or Pacific Islander, 41

(70.7%) were European/Caucasian/White, 2 (3.4%) were Latino/Latina/Hispanic, and 7 (12.1%) were of mixed race.

For the total sample, most students reported having a "B" grade average or higher ($\underline{n} = 86$, 91.5%) with the remainder indicating their grade average as "C" ($\underline{n} = 8$, 8.5%). No student indicated a grade of "D" or lower. Most students taking outdoor adventure education courses reported grades of "B" or higher ($\underline{n} = 31$, 86.1%); the remainder indicated a grade of "C" ($\underline{n} = 6$, 13.9%). 94.8% (n = 55) of the students not taking outdoor adventure education courses reported grades "B" or higher with the remaining 5.2% ($\underline{n} = 3$) reporting their grades as "C". There were no reported grades of "D" or lower in either of these groups.

A majority of the students (35.1%) were in tenth grade ($\underline{n} = 33$). Many of these tenth grade students ($\underline{n} = 26$) were enrolled in the Experiential Education course, one of the two outdoor adventure education courses offered at Friends Seminary. Twenty-seven students, or 28.7%, were in eleventh grade, 24 students (25.5%) were in ninth grade, and the remaining 10 students (10.6%) were in twelfth grade.

Of the 37 students in the eleventh or twelfth grade who participated in this study, 10 were enrolled in the Wilderness Course, the second outdoor adventure education course offered at Friends Seminary. Therefore, there were a total of 36 high school students (38.3% of the total sample) enrolled in outdoor adventure education courses during the Fall 2000 Semester.

Major Variables

Major variables of interest included scores derived from the MSCS, Life Events Survey, and the perceived risk-taking behaviors, level of outdoor experience, and perceived risk of outdoor activities scales included in the demographic portion of the questionnaire.

Baseline Data Collection

Means and standard deviations for major variables for the total sample, total sample by gender, and total sample by enrollment in an outdoor adventure education course are shown in Table 2. It is interesting to note there were no noticeable differences in any of the MSCS measures or other variables between males and females, or between those enrolled in or not enrolled in outdoor adventure education courses. However, the small divergences in self-concept that occurred followed those suggested in previous studies (Aries et al, 1998; Byrne & Shavelson, 1987; Crain, 1996; Crain & Bracken, 1994; Finkenberg, Shows & DiNucci, 1994; Marsh, Richards & Barnes, 1987).

The mean score on the Life Events Scale was 23.45 (SD = 10.25). The researcher multiplied this mean score by 4 to use as a reference for determining if there were any students who scored unusually high on the Life Events Survey when compared to their peers. No outliers were found using this method, and thus, all students were retained in the baseline sample. Females (M = 27.65, SD = 9.99) indicated having significantly more (t (92) = -4.42, p < .001) stressful life events than did males (M = 19.11, SD = 8.62).

Descriptive statistics were calculated for males and females who were enrolled in the outdoor adventure education courses as Hypotheses 8 and 9 specifically compare these groups. Means and standard deviations for major variables for males and females enrolled in the outdoor adventure education courses are displayed in Table 3.

Table 2

Means and Standard Deviations for Major Variables - Baseline Data Collection

	Total Sample	Gender		Adventure Education	
		Male	Female	In	Not In
Social Self-Concept					
M	76.52	76.49	76.55	77.22	76.09
SD	9.13	7.43	10.53	7.02	10.26
Competence Self-Concept					
M	75.97	75.33	76.55	75.44	76.29
SD	8.84	7.83	9.73	8.13	9.32
Affect Self-Concept					
M	73.65	75.91	71.57	75.75	72.34
SD	11.08	8.98	12.44	8.22	12.42
Academic Self-Concept					
M	74.11	72.53	75.55	72.22	72.34
SD	8.79	6.66	10.23	8.23	8.99
Family Self-Concept					
M	83.87	84.40	83.39	84.78	83.31
SD	12.19	10.36	13.76	9.54	13.64
Physical Self-Concept					
M	69.54	70.78	68.41	69.94	69.29
SD	9.94	9.78	10.05	9.21	10.44
Global Self-Concept					
M	453.60	455.38	451.96	455.28	452.55
SD	49.25	40.90	56.22	40.08	54.48
Perceived Risk of Outdoor Activities					
M	6.86	6.73	6.98	6.44	7.12
SD	3.10	3.19	3.05	3.09	3.11
Perceived Risk Taking Behaviors					
M	8.01	8.16	7.88	8.83	7.50
SD	2.20	2.35	2.06	2.05	2.15
Level of Outdoor Experience					
M	8.84	9.31	8.41	10.08	8.07
SD	3.90	3.75	4.02	4.24	3.49

Table 3

Baseline Means and Standard Deviations by Gender for Students Enrolled in Outdoor Adventure
Education Courses

Scale	Male		Female	
	M	SD	M	SD
Social	76.76	6.88	78.27	7.56
Competence	75.56	8.25	75.18	8.22
Affect	76.92	8.42	73.09	7.45
Academic	72.20	7.43	72.27	10.24
Family	83.64	9.46	87.36	9.65
Physical	71.64	9.48	66.09	7.60
Global	456.60	41.44	452.27	38.56
Perceived Risk of Outdoor Activities	6.32	2.87	6.73	3.69
Risk Taking Behaviors	8.84	2.01	8.82	2.23
Level of Outdoor Experience	10.64	4.04	8.82	4.60

A visual comparison of baseline scores on the MSCS showed no distinct differences between males and females who were taking outdoor adventure education courses. Although there was a difference in stressful life events between males ($\underline{M}$ = 19.64, $\underline{SD}$ = 8.96) and females ($\underline{M}$ = 24.00, $\underline{SD}$ = 8.94) who were taking outdoor adventure education classes, it was not significant.

Correlations among the major variables were calculated. As would be expected, there were many positive significant relationships between various subscales and the global scale of the MSCS

45

for the first measurement. Importantly, although there were significant relationships between Perceived Risk of Outdoor Activities, Previous Level of Outdoor Experience and the Physical subscale of the MSCS, none had r-values greater than .30. One condition for using a variable as a covariate is that the variable must show at least a moderate correlation with the dependent variable (Tabachnick & Fidell, 1996). Accordingly, these variables did not meet the criteria to be used a covariates.

The significant negative correlation between Perceived Risk and Risk Taking Behaviors (r = -.32, p < .001) indicates that as Perceived Risk of Outdoor Activities increases, Risk Taking Behaviors decrease. Additionally, the significant negative correlation (r = -.60, p < .001) between Perceived Risk of Outdoor Activities and Level of Outdoor Experience shows that those students reporting less outdoor experience believe outdoor activities to be more risky. Finally, the significant relationship (r = .37, p < .001) between Risk Taking Behaviors and Level of Outdoor Experience indicates those who take more risks report higher levels of outdoor experience. The correlation matrix for the baseline data collected is displayed in Table 4.

Table 4

Correlations Among Major Variables – Baseline Data

Scale	1	2	3	4	5	6	7	8	9
1. Social	--	--	--	--	--	--	--	--	--
2. Competence	.72**	--	--	--	--	--	--	--	--
3. Affect	.76**	.81**	--	--	--	--	--	--	--
4. Academic	.52**	.70**	.55**	--	--	--	--	--	--
5. Family	.46**	.61**	.60**	.56**	--	--	--	--	--
6. Physical	.62**	.65**	.70**	.46**	.44**	--	--	--	--
7. Global	.82**	.90**	.90**	.76**	.78**	.74**	--	--	--
8. Perceived Risk	-.10	-.05	-.12	.15	.11	-.26*	-.06	--	--
9. Risk Behavior	.07	.06	.07	-.10	-.01	.15	.05	-.32**	--
10. Outdoor Experience	-.04	.08	.04	-.02	-.05	.20*	.04	-.60**	.37**

Note. n = 94. *p < .05. **p < .001

Reliability analyses were conducted on each of the subscales, as well as the total scale for the MSCS. The subscales proved reliable, as Chronbach's alpha ranged from .88 (Academic Self-Concept) to .97 (Family Self-Concept). The Global Self-Concept scale was also reliable (α = .98).

Second Wave Data Collection

The second wave data collection session was conducted on October 18, 2000 following the procedures previously outlined. Of the 95 students who completed the baseline questionnaire, only 1 student failed to complete the second wave. Means and standard deviations for the total sample, the total sample by gender, and by whether or not a student was enrolled in an outdoor adventure education course are shown in Table 5.

A comparison using a paired t-test between the baseline scores and second wave scores for the total sample revealed no significant differences on the subscales and global scale of the MSCS or in reported Perceived Risk of Outdoor Activities, Risk Taking Behavior, or Level of Outdoor Experience. This was to be expected, as the outdoor trip component of the adventure education courses had not yet taken place. As at baseline, the standard deviation ($\underline{SD}$ = 12.00) for the second wave Life Events Survey was multiplied by 4 and used to evaluate the data for outliers. There were no scores more than 4 standard deviations away from the mean (M = 19.94); all students were retained in the sample.

For the total sample, students reported a significantly smaller score ($\underline{t}$ (93) = 3.82, $\underline{p}$ < .001) on the wave two Life Events Survey ($\underline{M}$ = 19.94, $\underline{SD}$ = 12.00). Perhaps these results reflected the return to a more structured environment (i.e., school) after summer vacation. Male students reported a significantly smaller Life Events Survey score ($\underline{t}$ (44) = 2.10, $\underline{p}$ < .05) on wave two ($\underline{M}$ = 16.24, $\underline{SD}$ = 10.50) than on wave one, as did females ($\underline{M}$ = 23.33, $\underline{SD}$ = 12.38, $\underline{t}$ (48) = 3.27, $\underline{p}$ < .01).

Table 5

Means and Standard Deviations for Major Variables - Second Wave Data Collection

		Gender		Adventure Education	
	Total Sample	Male	Female	In	Not In
Social Self-Concept					
M	76.59	77.16	76.06	77.50	76.02
SD	10.23	8.91	11.37	8.42	11.24
Competence Self-Concept					
M	75.80	75.40	76.16	75.42	76.03
SD	10.30	9.05	11.42	9.05	11.08
Affect Self-Concept					
M	74.39	76.80	72.18	75.50	73.71
SD	12.10	10.68	12.98	9.85	13.34
Academic Self-Concept					
M	74.51	73.47	75.47	72.81	75.57
SD	9.14	7.52	10.40	8.60	9.38
Family Self-Concept					
M	83.41	82.91	83.88	84.08	83.00
SD	12.65	11.08	14.05	10.52	13.89
Physical Self-Concept					
M	70.14	72.02	68.33	70.50	69.84
SD	9.95	9.62	10.02	9.96	10.03
Global Self-Concept					
M	454.80	457.76	452.08	455.81	454.17
SD	55.17	48.49	61.04	46.50	60.31
Perceived Risk of Outdoor Activities					
M	7.05	6.71	7.37	6.14	7.62
SD	3.44	3.33	3.55	3.27	3.45
Perceived Risk Taking Behaviors					
M	7.86	7.96	7.78	8.22	7.64
SD	2.13	2.13	2.14	2.00	2.19
Level of Outdoor Experience					
M	8.90	9.02	8.80	10.00	8.22
SD	3.61	3.43	3.80	3.36	3.62

There was also a significant difference ($\underline{t}$ (92) = -2.98, $\underline{p}$ < .01) on wave two Life Events Survey scores between males ($\underline{M}$ = 16.24, $\underline{SD}$ = 10.50) and females ($\underline{M}$ = 23.33, $\underline{SD}$ = 12.38). This may be attributed to the fact that adolescent females face more stressful situations in life than adolescent males and thus perceive more events as stressful (Rothenberg, 1995). Wave two descriptive statistics for males and females who were enrolled in outdoor adventure education courses are shown in Table 6.

Both males ($\underline{M}$ = 15.16, $\underline{SD}$ = 6.79), $\underline{t}$ (24) = 4.74, $\underline{p}$ < .001, and females ($\underline{M}$ = 17.36, $\underline{SD}$ = 5.95), $\underline{t}$ (10) = 3.46, $\underline{p}$ < .01, who were enrolled in outdoor adventure education courses scored significantly lower on the second wave Life Events Survey when compared to the baseline. Additionally, taken as a group, these students scored significantly lower on the second wave Life Events Survey ($\underline{t}$ (35) = 5.84, $\underline{p}$ < .001) than at baseline. They also reported significantly less Risk Taking Behaviors ($\underline{t}$ (35) = 2.51, $\underline{p}$ < .05). However, the mean difference is negligible (.61). Students not taking outdoor adventure education courses scored significantly higher on the second wave Affect scale ($\underline{t}$ (57) = -2.31, $\underline{p}$ < .05) when compared to the baseline.

Table 6

Second Wave Means and Standard Deviations by Gender for Students Enrolled in Outdoor Adventure Education Courses

Scale	Male		Female	
	M	SD	M	SD
Social	76.84	8.91	79.00	7.32
Competence	75.08	9.33	76.18	8.77
Affect	76.36	10.20	73.55	9.16
Academic	72.76	8.16	72.91	9.94
Family	81.68	10.51	89.55	8.65
Physical	73.00	9.52	64.82	8.86
Global	455.72	49.09	456.00	42.23
Perceived Risk of Outdoor Activities	5.60	2.77	7.36	4.08
Risk Taking Behaviors	8.44	2.00	7.73	2.00
Level of Outdoor Experience	10.12	3.17	9.73	3.90

Independent sample t-tests were used to compare means on major variables for those students taking outdoor adventure education courses and those students not taking these courses. Results are shown in Table 7. Students not in outdoor adventure education courses scored significantly higher on the Life Events Survey, Perceived Risk of Outdoor Activities, and Level of Outdoor Experience than those students enrolled in outdoor adventure education courses.

Table 7

Wave Two Differences Between Students Enrolled and Students Not Enrolled in Outdoor
Adventure Education Courses

	df	t
Social	92.0	-.68
Competence	92.0	.28
Affect	92.0	-.70
Academic	92.0	1.43
Family	92.0	-.40
Physical	92.0	-.31
Global	92.0	-.14
Life Events	87.1	3.14**
Perceived Risk of Outdoor Activities	92.0	2.06*
Risk Taking Behavior	92.0	-1.30
Level of Outdoor Experience	92.0	-2.35*

Note. The degrees of freedom for Life Events were smaller because Levene's Test for Homogeneity of Variance was significant, indicating unequal variances. The corrected statistics are reported. $*p < .05$. $**p < .01$

These differences may be possibly explained by participation by students in outdoor adventure education classroom activities. These activities were designed to prepare students for the outdoor trip component of the course. Student perceptions of the level of risk associated with outdoor activities were potentially affected by the preparatory experiences, as were their perceptions of level of outdoor experience. Additionally, these preparatory activities may have assisted students in confronting everyday life events, resulting in lower scores on the Life Events Survey.

A correlation matrix was constructed for major variables in wave two, and included baseline measures of Perceived Risk of Outdoor Activities, Risk Taking Behavior, and Level of Outdoor Experience. These last 3 variables were included to evaluate their use as covariates in future analyses. The correlation matrix is displayed in Table 8.

There were significant, positive correlations between the subscales of the MSCS and the Global Scale, which was expected. Interestingly, there were not significant relationships between the MSCS measures and Perceived Risk of Outdoor Activity, Risk Taking Behavior, or Level of Outdoor Experience. As such, these variables did not meet the criteria to be used as a covariate in the repeated measures ANCOVA analyses.

51

Reliability analyses were conducted on the subscales of the MSCS as well as the Global Scale. All were reliable, with Chronbach's alpha values ranging from .88 (Academic) to .97 (Family) for the subscales, and α = .98 for the Global Scale.

Table 8

Correlations Among Major Variables – Second Wave

Scale	1	2	3	4	5	6	7	8	9
1. Social	--	--	--	--	--	--	--	--	--
2. Competence	.79**	--	--	--	--	--	--	--	--
3. Affect	.80**	.82**	--	--	--	--	--	--	--
4. Academic	.62**	.79**	.66**	--	--	--	--	--	--
5. Family	.59**	.66**	.66**	.55**	--	--	--	--	--
6. Physical	.67**	.73**	.78**	.57**	.49**	--	--	--	--
7. Global	.87**	.93**	.93**	.80**	.79**	.82**	--	--	--
8. Perceived Risk	<.01	.06	-.04	.15	.08	-.19	.01	--	--
9. Risk Behavior	-.01	-.05	.04	-.13	-.03	.03	-.02	-.32**	--
10. Outdoor Experience	-.09	-.08	-.06	-.12	-.07	.15	-.05	-.60**	.37**

Note. Perceived Risk, Risk Behavior, and Outdoor Experience are baseline measures.

$\underline{n}$ = 94. **$\underline{p}$ < .001

Third Wave Data Collection

The final data collection occurred on December 18, 2000. This was immediately after the conclusion of the outdoor trip component of the adventure education courses. Data were collected using the same procedures as the first 2 sessions. All students completed the final survey, resulting in a final sample size of 94 subjects. Means and standard deviations for the total sample, the total sample by gender, and enrollment in an outdoor adventure education course are displayed in Table 9.

Table 9

Means and Standard Deviations for Major Variables - Third Wave Data Collection

	Total Sample	Gender		Adventure Education	
		Male	Female	In	Not In
Social Self-Concept					
M	76.89	76.02	77.69	77.33	76.62
SD	9.04	8.01	9.90	7.34	10.00
Competence Self-Concept					
M	75.78	74.73	76.73	75.22	76.12
SD	9.90	9.03	10.64	8.80	10.59
Affect Self-Concept					
M	74.81	76.31	73.43	74.94	74.72
SD	11.81	11.62	11.93	9.71	13.02
Academic Self-Concept					
M	75.50	74.40	76.51	73.03	77.03
SD	8.74	6.17	10.53	7.39	9.21
Family Self-Concept					
M	83.79	84.27	83.35	85.33	82.83
SD	12.57	11.98	13.19	11.07	13.42
Physical Self-Concept					
M	70.22	71.24	69.29	69.94	70.40
SD	10.24	9.65	10.77	10.04	10.45
Global Self-Concept					
M	456.99	456.98	457.00	455.81	457.72
SD	50.80	47.51	54.13	43.57	55.16
Perceived Risk of Outdoor Activities					
M	7.15	7.02	7.27	6.42	7.60
SD	3.18	3.39	3.01	3.20	3.11
Perceived Risk Taking Behaviors					
M	7.95	8.00	7.90	8.11	7.84
SD	2.09	2.26	1.94	2.12	2.08
Level of Outdoor Experience					
M	8.95	8.91	8.27	9.72	7.86
SD	3.64	3.45	3.47	3.07	3.52

Paired t-tests were used to compare the differences on the subscale and global scale of the MSCS, Perceived Risk of Outdoor Activities, Risk Taking Behavior, and Level of Outdoor Experience between baseline and third wave, and second and third wave measures for the total sample. Students reported a significant increase (t (93) = -2.53, p < .05) in Academic Self-Concept between the baseline and third wave measures. Additionally, there was a significant increase in Academic Self-Concept (t (93) = -2.39, p < .05) from the second to the third wave. However, the mean change in both comparisons was small, 1.39 and .99 respectively.

Changes in major variables between these measurement periods were also examined for males and females in the entire sample. Males reported significantly higher (t (44) = -2.81, p < .01) Academic Self-Concept on the third wave than at baseline.

The standard deviation (SD = 9.67) on the third wave Life Events Survey was multiplied by 4 to use as a method of evaluating students for possible outliers. As there were no scores above 4 standard deviations above the mean, all students were retained in the sample.

While comparing Life Events Survey scores for the total sample, there was a significant difference between baseline scores and wave three scores (t (93) = 5.12, p < .001) as indicated by a difference in means of 4.05. Both males (t (44) = -2.81, p< .01) and females (t (48) = 4.07, p< .001) in the total sample reported significantly fewer life events between wave one and wave three. Additionally, an independent samples t-test indicated females experienced significantly more stressful life events than did males (t (92) = -3.30, p = .001) as reported by the third wave Life Events Survey.

There were also significant differences for several of the variables based upon the status of enrollment in an outdoor education course. Those students who were enrolled in outdoor adventure education courses scored significantly lower (t (35) = 2.68, p < .05) on the Risk Taking Behavior scale from baseline to the third wave. The small mean difference was negligible. Those students not taking an outdoor adventure education course reported significantly higher Academic Self-Concept between baseline and the third wave (t (57) = -2.15, p < .05) as well as between the second and third wave measures (t (57) = -2.59, p < .05). However, the differences in means were small.

Those students not enrolled in outdoor adventure education courses reported a significantly lower score (t (57) = 4.36, p <.001) between baseline and wave three on the Life Events Survey. Interestingly, students who were enrolled in outdoor adventure education courses reported a significantly higher score (t (35) = -2.26, p < .05) on the third wave (M = 18.03, SD = 9.13) Life Events Survey than on the second wave (M = 15.83, SD = 6.54).

Additional independent sample t-tests were used to examine differences on third wave measures of major variables between those enrolled in and those not enrolled in outdoor adventure education courses. These results are shown in Table 10.

Table 10

Wave Three Differences Between Students Enrolled and Students Not Enrolled in Outdoor Adventure Education Courses

	df	t
Social	92	-.37
Competence	92	.43
Affect	92	-.09
Academic	92	2.21**
Family	92	-.94
Physical	92	.21
Global	92	.17
Life Events	92	1.17
Perceived Risk	92	1.78*
Risk Behavior	92	-.60
Outdoor Experience	92	-2.62***

Note. *$p < .10$. **$p < .05$. ***$p < .01$.

Although not significant at the $p < .05$ level, the difference in the Level of Perceived Risk of Outdoor Activities should be noted. Those students not enrolled in outdoor adventure education courses believed outdoor activities to be more risky than those taking an outdoor adventure education course ($t (92) = 1.78$, $p < .10$). This is not unreasonable, as those enrolled in the outdoor courses had encountered the risk of these activities and through this experience could downplay how much risk actually existed. Means and standard deviations for males and females enrolled in outdoor adventure education course for third wave measures of major variables are displayed in Table 11.

Table 11

Third Wave Means and Standard Deviations by Gender for Students Enrolled in Outdoor Adventure Education Courses

Scale	Male		Female	
	M	SD	M	SD
Social	76.76	7.37	78.64	7.45
Competence	74.80	8.76	76.18	9.24
Affect	76.20	10.14	72.09	8.38
Academic	72.88	6.63	73.36	9.25
Family	83.28	11.41	90.00	89.04
Physical	72.04	9.68	65.18	9.59
Global	455.96	46.24	455.45	38.91
Perceived Risk of Outdoor Activities	6.12	3.24	7.09	3.14
Risk Taking Behaviors	8.24	2.11	7.82	2.23
Level of Outdoor Experience	10.28	3.10	8.45	2.70

Independent sample and paired sample t-tests were conducted to compare female and male scores on the third wave major variables for those students enrolled in outdoor adventure education courses. Females reported significantly higher (t (34) = -1.73, p < .10) Family Self-Concept than males. Males reported significantly higher Physical Self-Concept (t (34) = 1.96, p < .10) and greater Level of Outdoor Experience (t (34) = 1.69, p < .10). Females indicated experiencing significantly fewer stressful life events between baseline and wave three ($\underline{t}$ (10) = 2.01, $\underline{p}$ < .10). Males indicated a significant increase in life events from wave two to wave three ($\underline{t}$ (24) = -2.22, $\underline{p}$ < .05), a significant decrease in life events from baseline to wave three ($\underline{t}$ (24) = 1.86, $\underline{p}$ < .10), and a significant decrease in Risk Taking Behaviors from wave one to wave three ($\underline{t}$ (24) = 2.00, $\underline{p}$ < .10).

A correlation matrix was constructed for the entire sample for third wave major variables. This appears in Table 12. The significant correlations among the subscales and the Global scale of the MSCS are to be expected, as they have been shown to be modestly intercorrelated (Bracken, 1996).

The significant correlations between Physical Self-Concept and Perceived Risk of Outdoor Activities ($\underline{r}$ = -.22, $\underline{p}$ < .05) suggests those with higher Physical Self-Concept believe there is less risk associated with outdoor activities. The belief that one has the physical ability to cope with the challenges of the outdoor environment most likely explains this relationship. Perceived risks may appear less likely to have consequences to those with greater perceived physical ability, and thus affect perceptions of risk associated with outdoor activities.

Table 12

Correlations Among Major Variables – Third Wave

Scale	1	2	3	4	5	6	7	8	9
1. Social	--	--	--	--	--	--	--	--	--
2. Competence	.78**	--	--	--	--	--	--	--	--
3. Affect	.79**	.78**	--	--	--	--	--	--	--
4. Academic	.69**	.73**	.61**	--	--	--	--	--	--
5. Family	.47**	.45**	.48**	.46**	--	--	--	--	--
6. Physical	.65**	.68**	.76**	.52**	.30**	--	--	--	--
7. Global	.88**	.89**	.90**	.80**	.67**	.79**	--	--	--
8. Perceived Risk	-.06	.02	-.09	.08	.10	-.22*	-.03	--	--
9. Risk Behavior	.05	-.01	.04	-.08	.06	.02	.02	-.32**	--
10. Outdoor Experience	-.01	.02	.03	-.08	.03	.21*	.05	-.60**	.37**

Note. Perceived Risk, Risk Behavior, and Outdoor Experience are baseline measures. $\underline{n}$ = 94.
*$\underline{p}$ < .05. **$\underline{p}$ < .001.

Additionally, those students with greater Levels of Outdoor Experience reported higher levels of Physical Self-Concept ($\underline{r}$ = .21, $\underline{p}$ < .05). This may be related to the physical nature of outdoor pursuits, and the effects that participating in physical activities in the outdoor may have on self-concept. Also, those with higher levels of Physical Self-Concept may find themselves more attracted to outdoor experiences than those with lower levels, possibly explaining this difference. Once again, none of the correlations among these variables met the criteria for use as a covariate in repeated measures ANCOVA analyses.

Reliability analyses were conducted for the subscales and Global scale of the MSCS. Chronbach's alphas ranged from $\alpha = .88$ (Academic Self-Concept) to $\alpha = .98$ (Global Self-Concept) indicating high reliability.

A correlation matrix was constructed for students enrolled in an outdoor adventure education course to determine if it was appropriate to use Perceived Risk of Outdoor Activities, Risk Taking Behavior, and Level of Outdoor Experience as covariates (See Table 13).

Upon examination of the correlations for those students enrolled in outdoor adventure education courses, only Previous Level of Outdoor Experience and Competence Self-Concept from the first measure had an r-value greater than or equal to .30. Therefore, this will be the only covariate used when appropriate in analyzing Hypothesis 8.

Table 13

Correlations Among Major Variables for Students Enrolled in Outdoor Adventure Education Courses

	Perceived Risk	Risk Behavior	Outdoor Experience
Social 1	.10	<.01	-.03
Competence 1	-.14	.06	.32
Affect 1	-.17	.02	.27
Academic 1	.03	-.10	.23
Family 1	-.03	.10	.20
Physical 1	.05	<.01	.19
Global 1	-.04	.02	.26
Social 2	.24	-.16	-.06
Competence 2	.13	-.11	.10
Affect 2	.08	-.01	.06
Academic 2	.08	-.05	.11
Family 2	.12	-.01	-.01
Physical 2	.09	-.06	.13
Global 2	.15	-.07	.07
Social 3	.13	-.12	.02
Competence 3	.10	.04	.13
Affect 3	.01	-.01	.19
Academic 3	-.01	-.08	.21
Family 3	.03	.05	.10
Physical 3	.01	-.09	.17
Global 3	.05	-.03	.17

Hypotheses Testing

All hypotheses were examined using repeated measures ANCOVA analyses. The baseline measure of the MSCS scale was used as the covariate for all hypotheses. Additionally, the baseline measure of Previous Level of Outdoor Experience was used as the covariate when examining differences between Competence Self-Concept of males and females enrolled in the outdoor adventure education courses (Hypothesis 8).

Hypothesis One

It was hypothesized that students enrolled in outdoor adventure education courses would have significantly greater change in Global Self-Concept than those students not enrolled in outdoor adventure education courses. Differences in change in Global Self-Concept between students enrolled in outdoor adventure education courses and students not enrolled in these courses were examined. Levene's Test of Equality of Variances was significant for the third wave Global Self-Concept measure (F (1,92) = 6.09, p < .05), indicating the assumption of homogeneity of variance for the between-subjects test was not tenable.

To rectify this situation, the base ten logarithms were calculated for all Global Self-Concept measures and were used in a repeated measures ANCOVA analysis. Using this procedure, Levene's Test for homogeneity of variance proved tenable (F (1,86) = .11, p = .75 for the base ten log of second wave Global Self-Concept, F (1,86) = 3.62, p = .06 for the base ten log of third wave Global Self-Concept). The covariate, the base ten log of baseline Global Self-Concept, was significant (F (1,85) = 413.18, p < .001). However, the test of between-subjects effects yielded a non-significant result (F (1,85) = .09, p = .76). Therefore, this hypothesis was not supported, as there were no significant differences in change in Global Self-Concept between those enrolled in outdoor adventure education courses and those not enrolled in these courses.

Hypothesis Two

Hypothesis two stated that students in outdoor adventure education courses would have significantly greater change in Physical Self-Concept than students not enrolled in outdoor adventure education courses. The assumption of homogeneity of variance was tenable (wave two Physical Self-Concept: F (1,92) = .02, p = .88, wave three Physical Self-Concept: F (1,92) = .11, p = .74), and the baseline measure of Physical Self-Concept was significant as the covariate (F (1,91) = 363.24, p < .001). The repeated measure ANCOVA did not yield a significant result (F (1,91) = .252, p = .62). Therefore, hypothesis two was not supported.

Hypothesis Three

There was no significant difference in change in Affect Self-Concept between students in outdoor adventure education courses and students not in these courses; therefore hypothesis three was not supported. There was no significant change in repeated measures Affect Self-Concept (F (1,91) = 2.75, p = .10) after adjusting for baseline Affect Self-Concept, which was significant (F

(1,91) = 272.84, $\underline{p}$ < .001). Homogeneity of variance was tenable (wave two Affect Self-Concept: $\underline{F}$ (1,92) = 1.06, $\underline{p}$ = .31, wave three Affect Self-Concept: $\underline{F}$ (1,92) = 3.31, $\underline{p}$ = .07).

Hypothesis Four

The fourth hypothesis predicted a greater change in Competence Self-Concept for students taking outdoor adventure education courses than those not taking outdoor adventure education courses. This hypothesis was also not supported, as the results of the repeated measures ANCOVA were not significant ($\underline{F}$ (1,92) = .002, $\underline{p}$ = .97). Baseline Competence Self-Concept was significant as a covariate ($\underline{F}$ (1,92) = 301.91, $\underline{p}$ < .001) and homogeneity of variance was tenable (wave two Competence Self-Concept: F (1,92) = .71, $\underline{p}$ = .40, wave three Competence Self-Concept: F (1,92) = 3.53, $\underline{p}$ = .06).

Hypothesis Five

This researcher posited students enrolled in outdoor adventure education would have a greater change in Social Self-Concept than students not enrolled in these courses. Hypothesis Five was not supported; there was a non-significant result of the repeated measure ANCOVA ($\underline{F}$ (1,91) = .01, $\underline{p}$ = .91). Levene's Test was not significant for the second or third wave measures of Social Self-Concept ($\underline{F}$ (1,92) = 1.36, $\underline{p}$ = .25, $\underline{F}$ (1,92) = 1.02, $\underline{p}$ = .31, respectively). The covariate proved significant for this hypothesis ($\underline{F}$ (1,92) = 262.50, $\underline{p}$ < .001).

Hypothesis Six

This hypothesis predicted the change in Family Self-Concept between those not in outdoor adventure education courses and those in these courses. This hypothesis was also not supported, as the repeated measures ANCOVA yielded a non-significant result ($\underline{F}$ (1,91) = .16, $\underline{p}$ = .69). As with the previous hypotheses, the covariate was significant (F (1,91) = 234.19, p < .001), and the homogeneity of variance was tenable ($\underline{F}$ (1,92) = .363, $\underline{p}$ = .55, $\underline{F}$ (1,92) = 1.85, $\underline{p}$ = .18).

Hypothesis Seven

This hypothesis suggested that there would be a significant difference in change in Academic Self-Concept between the aforementioned groups. The repeated measures ANCOVA did not support this hypothesis ($\underline{F}$ (1,92) = .69, $\underline{p}$ = .41). Homogeneity of variance was tenable ($\underline{F}$ (1,92) = .78, $\underline{p}$ = .38 for wave one Academic Self-Concept, $\underline{F}$ (1,92) = 4.52, $\underline{p}$ = .17 for wave two Academic Self-Concept). The covariate proved significant ($\underline{F}$ (1,91) = 262.39, $\underline{p}$ < .001).

61

<u>Hypothesis Eight</u>

The eighth hypothesis stated that females enrolled in outdoor adventure education courses would have greater change in Physical, Affect, Academic and Competence Self-Concept than males enrolled in outdoor adventure education courses. Baseline measures of the corresponding MSCS scale were used as a covariate in all analyses; all were significant. All analyses met the assumption of homogeneity of variance; Levene's tests were not significant. Additionally, Previous Level of Outdoor Experience was included as a covariate in the analysis of Competence Self-Concept, and it was significant (F (1,32) = 4.79, p < .01). There were no significant differences in change in these domains of self-concept between females and males, as may be seen in Table 14. Thus, this hypothesis was not supported.

<u>Hypothesis 9</u>

This hypothesis posited that males enrolled in outdoor adventure education courses would have significantly greater gains in Social and Family Self-Concept than females in these courses. The repeated measures ANCOVA analysis for Social Self-Concept was not significant (F (1,33) = .18, p = .68) although the covariate was significant (F (1,33) = 101.71, p < .001). The assumption of homogeneity of variance was met for this test as well (second wave Social Self-Concept: F (1,340 = .14, p = .71, third wave Social Self-Concept: F (1,34) = .48, p = .50). This hypothesis was not supported for Social Self-Concept.

Table 14

Repeated Measures ANCOVA Results for Hypothesis Eight

Analysis	df	F
Physical Self-Concept		
Physical Self-Concept (Covariate)	1	121.03**
Gender	1	2.13
S Between-Groups Error	33	
Affect Self-Concept		
Affect Self-Concept (Covariate)	1	96.85**
Gender	1	.06
S Between-Groups Error	33	
Academic Self-Concept		
Academic Self-Concept (Covariate)	1	176.84**
Gender	1	.05
S Between-Groups Error	33	
Competence Self-Concept		
Competence Self-Concept (Covariate)	1	146.34**
Previous Level of Outdoor Experience	1	4.79*
Gender	1	.47
S Between-Groups Error	32	

$*p < .05.$ $**p < .001.$

There was a significant difference in gain of Family Self-Concept for males and females enrolled in outdoor adventure education courses. Males had significantly greater gain ($F_{(1,33)}$ = 4.01, $p < .05$) in Family Self-Concept using the baseline measure as the covariate ($F_{(1,33)}$ = 82.73, $p < .001$). Additionally, the assumption of homogeneity of variance was tenable (second wave Family Self-Concept: $F_{(1,34)}$ = 1.64, $p = .21$, third wave Family Self-Concept: $F_{(1,34)}$ = .006, $p = .938$). Figure 2 shows the change in Family Self-Concept.

Figure 2

Change in Family Self-Concept for Students In Outdoor Adventure Education Courses Between Males and Females

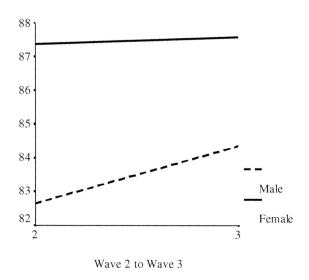

Wave 2 to Wave 3

The ninth hypothesis was supported as a result; males enrolled in outdoor adventure education courses showed significantly greater gains in Family Self-Concept than females enrolled in these courses.

Supplementary Analyses

Some previous studies examined the effects of participating in outdoor adventure education courses on students who were categorized as having Low Self-Concept (Marsh & Richards, 1988; McDonald & Howe, 1989; Minor & Elrod, 1994). However, these students also were characterized by other factors such as low academic achievement, status as a juvenile offender, and experiencing physical, mental or emotional abuse. There has been no examination of typical students characterized as having Low Self-Concept who participate in outdoor adventure education courses. Therefore, several supplementary analyses were conducted to determine if there were any differences in gains in the domains or global self-concept between students who indicated having High Global Self-Concept or Low Global Self-Concept. In order to determine if students had high or low Global Self-Concept, the sum of the Global Self-Concept scores for all three waves was determined. The median score ($\underline{Mdn}$ = 1352.50) of this sum was used as the basis of separating the sample into high or low self-concept groups (i.e., high self-concept $\geq$ 1352.51, low self-concept $\leq$ 1352.50). This grouping variable was used in the analyses of the domains of self-concept as well, as Global Self-Concept has been noted as highly correlated with each of the domains (Bracken, 1996).

Two comparisons were conducted for each of the domains and Global Self-Concept using the repeated measure ANCOVA with corresponding baseline measure as the covariate. The first comparison examined the differences, if any, between those students with low self-concept taking and not taking outdoor adventure education courses. The same analyses were conducted comparing like groups for those students with high self-concept.

The second comparison used only those students taking outdoor adventure education courses. Differences in the change of self-concept, if any, between student with high self-concept and students with low self-concept were examined. The sample size for these analyses was 36 students.

Results

The results of the repeated measures ANCOVA using the corresponding baseline MSCS measure as a covariate indicated no significant differences between students taking outdoor adventure education courses with high self-concept and students not taking these courses with high self-concept. Additionally, there were no significant differences between like groups for students with low self-concepts. Descriptive statistics before controlling for baseline differences are shown in Table 15. Results of the repeated measures ANCOVA are shown in Table 16. Levene's test of homogeneity of variance proved tenable for each of these analyses. These findings suggest there are no noticeable differences in gains in self-concept for those students with high or low self-concept enrolled in adventure education courses when compared to students not enrolled in these courses with similar self-concepts.

Table 15

Descriptive Statistics for First Supplementary Analyses

High or Low Group		Taking Outdoor Course	M	SD	n
Low	Global Self-Concept 2	No	403.46	43.41	26
		Yes	426.33	22.84	21
		Total	413.68	37.19	47
	Global Self-Concept 3	No	410.38	33.94	26
		Yes	429.38	23.29	21
		Total	418.87	30.87	47
High	Global Self-Concept 2	No	495.38	35.47	32
		Yes	497.07	39.15	15
		Total	495.91	36.26	47
	Global Self-Concept 3	No	496.19	35.48	32
		Yes	492.80	38.18	15
		Total	495.11	35.98	47

The second set of analyses compared only those students enrolled in the outdoor adventure education courses. Students with low self-concept were compared to those students with high self-concept to determine if there were significant differences in change in the domains of self-concept as well as Global Self-Concept. The analyses indicated there were significant differences in change in 4 domains of self-concept (Social, Competence, Academic, Family) as well as Global Self-Concept.

Table 16

Analysis of Covariance for Students Taking Adventure Education Courses vs. Students Not Taking Adventure Education Courses Grouped by High or Low Self-Concept

Scale	n	df	F
Global Self-Concept			
High	47	1	.01
Low	47	1	.80
Social Self-Concept			
High	47	1	.14
Low	47	1	1.96
Competence Self-Concept			
High	47	1	.13
Low	47	1	.57
Affect Self-Concept			
High	47	1	1.01
Low	47	1	.35
Academic Self-Concept			
High	47	1	.70
Low	47	1	.06
Family Self-Concept			
High	47	1	1.07
Low	47	1	.01
Physical Self-Concept			
High	47	1	.02
Low	47	1	.04

Note. df for error for all analyses were 44.

Descriptive statistics for these groups before controlling for baseline differences for Global Self-Concept are shown in Table 17. Levene's test for homogeneity of variance proved tenable, and the test of between-subjects effects was significant (F (1,33) = 5.47, $p < .05$).

Table 17

Descriptive Statistics for Those Enrolled in Outdoor Adventure Education Courses by High or Low Global Self-Concept

	High or Low Global Self-Concept	M	SD	n
Global Self-Concept 2	Low	426.33	22.84	21
	High	497.07	39.15	15
	Total	455.81	46.50	36
Global Self-Concept 3	Low	429.38	23.29	21
	High	492.80	38.18	15
	Total	455.81	43.57	36

Figure 3 depicts the change in Global Self-Concept for these two groups, after adjusting for differences in baseline Global Self-Concept. In addition, Figure 3 indicates that students with High Global Self-Concept decreased in score between waves 2 and 3 while students with Low Global Self-Concept increased during the same time period. The difference is significant (F (1,33) = 5.47, $p < .05$).

Figure 3

Change in Global Self-Concept for Students In Outdoor Adventure Education Courses with High and Low Global Self-Concept

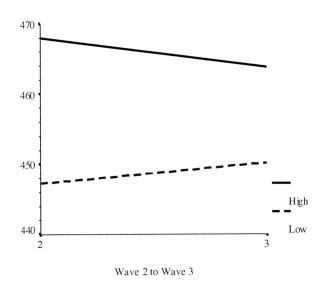

Wave 2 to Wave 3

There was also a significant difference in change in Social Self-Concept. Descriptive statistics before controlling for baseline differences are shown in Table 18. Homogeneity of variance was tenable, as Levene's tests were not significant. The repeated measure ANCOVA was significant (F (1,33) = 18.61, p < .001), indicating differences in change in Social Self-Concept between students with high and low self-concept taking adventure education courses. Figure 4 shows the change from wave two to three, after adjusting for differences in baseline Social Self-Concept.

Table 18

Descriptive Statistics for Those Enrolled in Outdoor Adventure Education Courses for Social Self-Concept by High or Low Global Self-Concept

	High or Low Global Self-Concept	M	SD	n
Social Scale 2	Low	71.26	4.90	19
	High	84.47	5.49	17
	Total	77.50	8.42	36
Social Scale 3	Low	72.21	5.00	19
	High	83.06	4.88	17
	Total	77.33	7.34	36

Students with High Global Self-Concept showed a decrease in Social Self-Concept from wave 2 to wave 3, while students with Low Global Self-Concept showed an increase during this time period. However, as Figure 4 indicates, even though there was a significant difference between the groups, the gains and losses were small after adjusting for baseline Social Self-Concept scores. The difference becomes significant when the combined effects of the small gain in Social Self-Concept for the Low Global Self-Concept group are combined with the small decrease in Social Self-Concept by the High Self-Concept group.

Figure 4

Change in Social Self-Concept for Students In Outdoor Adventure Education Courses with High and Low Global Self-Concept

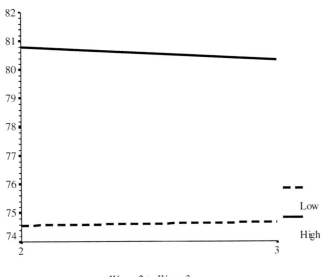

Wave 2 to Wave 3

Students in the Low Self-Concept group showed significantly greater gains ($\underline{F}$ (1,33) = 6.50, $\underline{p}$ < .05) in Competence Self-Concept than students with High Self-Concepts. Students in the latter group actually showed a decrease in Competence Self-Concept after controlling for differences in baseline Competence Self-Concept. Descriptive statistics for these groups before controlling for the baseline scores are shown in Table 19. Figure 5 provides a visual description of the difference between these groups after controlling for baseline Competence Self-Concept.

Table 19

Descriptive Statistics for Those Enrolled in Outdoor Adventure Education Courses for Competence

Self-Concept by High or Low Global Self-Concept

	High or Low Global Self-Concept	M	SD	n
Competence Scale 2	Low	69.86	4.42	21
	High	83.20	8.11	15
	Total	75.42	9.05	36
Competence Scale 3	Low	70.10	4.53	21
	High	82.40	8.35	15
	Total	75.22	8.80	36

Figure 5

Change in Competence Self-Concept for Students In Outdoor Adventure Education Courses with

High and Low Global Self-Concept

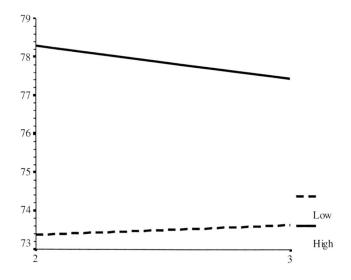

Wave 2 to Wave 3

As may be seen from Figure 5, the small increase in Competence Self-Concept by students with Low Global Self-Concept combined with the somewhat larger decrease by students with High Global Self-Concept explains the significant difference.

After controlling for baseline differences in Academic Self-Concept, there was a significant difference between students with Low Self-Concept and students with High Self-Concept (F (1,33) = 7.72, p < .01). The test for homogeneity of variance was tenable, as Levene's test yielded no significant results (second wave Academic Self-Concept: F (1,34) = .08, p = .79, third wave Academic Self-Concept: F (1,34) = .02, p = .89). Descriptive statistics before controlling for baseline differences are shown in Table 20.

Table 20

Descriptive Statistics for Those Enrolled in Outdoor Adventure Education Courses for Academic Self-Concept by High and Low Global Self-Concept

	High or Low Global Self-Concept	M	SD	n
Academic Scale 2	Low	67.62	4.84	21
	High	80.07	7.37	15
	Total	72.81	8.60	36
Academic Scale 3	Low	68.57	3.49	21
	High	79.27	6.91	15
	Total	73.03	7.39	36

As depicted in Figure 6, students in the Low Self-Concept group showed an increase in Academic Self-Concept from wave 2 to wave 3, after controlling for baseline Academic Self-Concept. Additionally, those students in the High Self-Concept group indicated a slight decrease from wave 2 to wave 3 after controlling for baseline Academic Self-Concept scores. Although the Low Self-Concept students scored lower than High Self-Concept students, the positive change in Academic Self-Concept is notable.

Figure 6

Change in Academic Self-Concept for Students In Outdoor Adventure Education Courses with High and Low Global Self-Concept

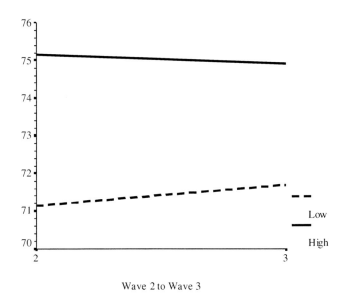

Wave 2 to Wave 3

The final significant finding regards changes in Family Self-Concept. Unlike the differences previously discussed above, students with High Self-Concept showed greater positive change in Family Self-Concept than students with Low Self-Concept ($\underline{F}$ (1,33) = 18.02, $\underline{p}$ < .001). Descriptive statistics before controlling for baseline Family Self-Concept are shown in Table 21. Levene's test for homogeneity of variance proved tenable, as there were no significant findings.

Table 21

Descriptive Statistics for Those Enrolled in Outdoor Adventure Education Courses for Family Self-Concept by High and Low Global Self-Concept

	High or Low Global Self-Concept	M	SD	n
Family Scale 2	Low	75.76	5.11	17
	High	91.53	8.26	19
	Total	84.08	10.52	36
Family Scale 3	Low	75.29	5.42	17
	High .	94.32	5.64	19
	Total	85.33	11.07	36

As may be seen in Figure 7, students with High Global Self-Concept indicate a positive change from wave 2 to wave 3 after adjusting for baseline difference in Family Self-Concept. Students with Low Global Self-Concept indicate a decrease in Family Self-Concept from wave 2 to wave 3 after controlling for initial differences in Family Self-Concept.

Figure 7

Change in Family Self-Concept for Students In Outdoor Adventure Education Courses with High and Low Global Self-Concept

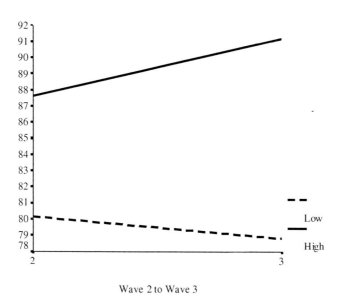

Wave 2 to Wave 3

There were no significant differences between students with High Global Self-Concept and students with Low Global Self-Concept in either Affect Self-Concept or Physical Self-Concept (F $(1,33) = .66$, $p = .42$, F $(1,33) = 3.13$, $p = .09$, respectively). Figure 8 shows the differences in Affect Self-Concept between these groups of students after adjusting for baseline scores. As seen in Figure 8, both groups of students show decreases in Affect Self-Concept of roughly the same magnitude after controlling for baseline Affect Self-Concept. The decrease in score for both groups was negligible as well (less than one point on the scale).

Figure 8

Change in Affect Self-Concept for Students In Outdoor Adventure Education Courses with High
and Low Global Self-Concept

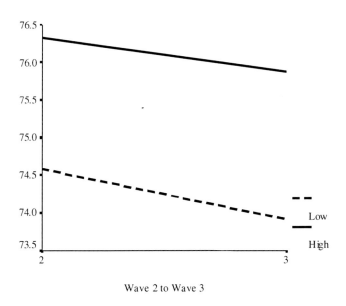

Wave 2 to Wave 3

The differences in Physical Self-Concept were not significant at the $p \leq .05$ level. However,
they were significant at the $p \leq .10$ level (F (1,33) = 3.13). Figure 9 shows that after adjusting for
baseline scores, students with High Global Self-Concept indicate a slight increase in Physical Self-
Concept. This figure also indicates that students with Low Global Self-Concept indicate a decrease
in Physical Self-Concept. However, the magnitude in change in each group is relatively small.

Figure 9

Change in Physical Self-Concept for Students In Outdoor Adventure Education Courses with High and Low Global Self-Concept

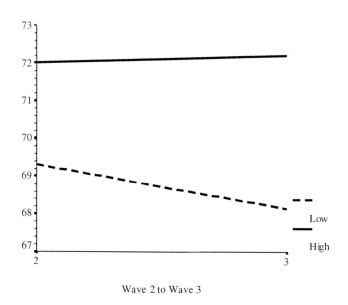

Wave 2 to Wave 3

The testing of the stated hypotheses as well as the supplementary analyses resulted in several significant findings in various components of self-concept of students. The findings have implications for the delivery of outdoor adventure education programs in academic settings. A discussion of the findings and their implications, as well as recommendations for future research are discussed in the next chapter.

CHAPTER V

DISCUSSION

The development of self-concept has been documented as an important component of adolescent social and emotional growth (Crain & Bracken, 1994). The use of peer groups as a means of evaluating the various facets of self-concept is an important point because peers play a significant role in adolescent life (Walker & Green, 1986). As adolescents generally spend a large amount of time in the school environment with their peers, it is imperative that educators and administrators learn the ways in which academic programs may impact adolescent self-concept. The inclusion of outdoor adventure education programs in traditional academic settings has many purposes, and their potential to affect the self-concept of students may be one of the most important outcomes. The purpose of this study was to examine that impact on a select group of high school students.

Hypotheses

Increased self-concept has been cited as one of the potential benefits of participating in outdoor adventure education activities (Hattie, et al., 1997). Previous researchers have found significant changes in Global Self-Concept as well as the domains of self-concept as a result of high school students participating in outdoor adventure education courses (Finkenberg et al., 1994; Gillett et al, 1991; Luckner, 1989; Marsh et al., 1986). This researcher found no significant difference between changes in Global Self-Concept for both female and male high school students ages 13 to 18 enrolled in outdoor adventure education courses and students not enrolled in these courses. This study supports the contention that General or Global Self-Concept is reasonably stable over a four-month time period. Changes in Global Self-Concept are less likely to occur than changes in the various domains of self-concept over a similar time period. Additionally, the findings of this study reflect those of previous researchers' that suggested the sum change in the domains of self-concept result in changes in Global Self-Concept (Bracken, 1992; Byrne & Shavelson, 1986; Marsh et al., 1988; Shavelson et al., 1976).

Unlike previous studies, this researcher found no significant differences in any of the domains of self-concept between high school students enrolled in outdoor adventure education courses and students not enrolled in these courses. Other researchers found that students of similar ages to those in this study who participated in outdoor adventure education courses had significant changes in various domains of self-concept, including: Physical, Social, Academic, Parents,

79

Problem Solving and Identity among others (Hattie et al., 1997; Lambert et al., 1978; Luckner, 1989; Marsh & Richards, 1988; Marsh, Richards & Barnes, 1986; McDonald & Howe, 1989). It should be noted that researchers have confirmed the general stability of self-concept during adolescence, which allows for the comparison of multiple age groups (Crain, 1994; Marsh, 1993).

The nature of the outdoor adventure education courses examined in this study were different than those in previous studies, and may have affected the findings. Students in this study participated in two short-term (three days each) outdoor experiences spread over the course of four months. The outdoor experience component of other studies were usually longer in length and of continuous duration. The extent of the outdoor experiences in this study may have affected the lack of change in Global Self-Concept and the domains of self-concept. Longer courses have been found to have greater effects than short-term courses (Hattie et al., 1997). These two factors (general stability of Global Self-Concept and its domains over time, and the short duration of program) may explain the lack of significant change in self-concept between students enrolled in outdoor adventure education courses and those not enrolled in these courses examined in this study. In addition, the intensity of these outdoor adventure education experiences for the group of students examined in this study may have affected the findings. Perhaps the outdoor components were not challenging enough to cause self-evaluation and adjustment of Global Self-Concept or any of the domains of self-concept. The findings from this study are not unlike those reporting on short-term outdoor adventure education courses (Hattie, et al.).

When examining differences in self-concept between males and females enrolled in outdoor adventure education courses, this researcher found a significant difference in gain in Family Self-Concept favoring males. Females have been posited to possess higher self-concepts than males in areas concerning social relationships such as with friends and family. The social interaction needed for teamwork and for the understanding of others that occurs on outdoor adventure education courses may have a greater affect in males' perceptions of their families by allowing them to transfer these experiences to family life. Other researchers examining the effects of outdoor adventure education programs have generally not used instruments that include a scale for Family Self-Concept. Bracken (2000) notes this as a discrepancy in many existing measures.

As indicated earlier, previous research has found little difference between self-concept and its domains between males and females. The differences that do exist tend to mirror stereotypical beliefs about self-concept (e.g., males have greater physical self-concept, females have greater social self-concept) (Crain & Bracken, 1994; Wilgenbush & Merrill, 1999). There were no significant differences in gains in the other domains of self-concept between males and females taking outdoor adventure education courses. Other studies have examined the effects of outdoor adventure education programs on self-concept, but did not report differences between males and females taking these courses. These studies typically compared same gender groups who were taking or not taking outdoor adventure education courses, or reported on mixed gender groups (Finkenberg, et al., 1994; Gillett et al., 1991; Hazelworth & Wilson, 1990). This research supports previous findings suggesting there is little difference between adolescent male and female gains in self-concept within the context of outdoor adventure education.

Supplementary Analyses

Although earlier studies examining outdoor adventure education courses and their effects on adolescent self-concept have generally provided mixed results, several studies investigating outdoor adventure education with students identified as having low self-concept have produced positive findings (Marsh & Richards, 1988; McDonald & Howe, 1989; Minor & Elrod, 1994). However, mitigating factors such as physical, mental or emotional abuse, status as a juvenile offender, or identification as having poor academic performance potentially influenced the self-concepts of participants in these studies. Thus, it is important to evaluate how outdoor adventure education programs affect students who are characterized as having Low Global Self-Concept when compared to their peers who have none of the mitigating factors mentioned above.

The comparison of students characterized as having Low Global Self-Concept and those having High Global Self-Concept has not been discussed in previous studies. Some researchers, however, have examined students with low achievement. Marsh and Richards (1988) found increased self-concept among low achieving youth after participation in an Outward Bound style course. McDonald and Howe (1989) reported on children with low self-concept, and found increased self-concept as a result of participating in four one-hour long outdoor adventure education activities. The supplementary data analyses of this study thus contribute to the present state of knowledge by comparing students with Low and High Global Self-Concept who were exposed to the same experiences.

There was a significant difference ($p < .05$) in gain in Global Self-Concept between students in this study who were categorized as having High Self-Concept and students having Low Self-Concept who were enrolled in the outdoor adventure education courses. Students with Low Global Self-Concept showed a slight gain in Global Self-Concept while those with High Global Self-Concept indicated a slight decrease after controlling for baseline differences (see Figure 3). The outdoor adventure education courses appear to have made a greater impact on some of the various domains of self-concept for Low Global Self-Concept students, which led to their gain in Global Self-Concept.

The findings of this study indicate a similar pattern of increased Social Self-Concept, Competence Self-Concept, and Academic Self-Concept for students having Low Global Self-Concept. The outdoor adventure education experience may provide an environment of "equal footing" for students who may not normally associate with one another. These courses offer a forum to interact with others in ways outside of the everyday experience such as the classroom or neighborhood. Outdoor adventure education courses often require students to work together to reach a common goal, which enables social interaction to occur (Hattie et al., 1997). For those students with low self-concept, the ability to interact with others in an environment of equality provided by outdoor adventure education courses may allow them to feel better about themselves. Particularly, it may affect their interactions with others, how they are accepted by fellow students, and the sense of positive social acceptance. In addition, it may allow them to experiment with and confirm identities they wish to establish, particularly with a group of peers. Students with high self-concept may not be affected to the same extent as students with low self-concept. In fact, students with high self-concept may indicate decreased Social Self-Concept, as they are either required to interact with students who may not be "cool" or acceptable in student society or in an environment in which their senses of self are challenged.

Previous studies have reported differences in Competence Self-Concept and related areas between those taking outdoor adventure education courses and those not taking outdoor adventure education courses. Additionally, differences were found to exist in pretest/posttest studies examining students taking outdoor adventure education courses (Gillett et al., 1991; Hattie et al., 1997; Hazelworth & Wilson, 1990). However, no intergroup results have been reported regarding Competence Self-Concept.

The nature of outdoor adventure education courses lends itself to the increase in Competence Self-Concept in students with Low Global Self-Concept in much the same manner as does Social Self-Concept. Outdoor adventure education courses may include activities such as rock climbing and backpacking that usually require individuals to actively participate. In addition, outdoor adventure education activities provide immediate feedback to the success or lack of success of the participant. Pre-trip practice and preparation, the repetitive nature of activities of daily living in the outdoors, and the opportunity to re-try activities such as tying knots or climbing a particular route may affect Competence Self-Concept, especially for those whose self-concept is low to start.

As Luckner stated, "Mastery of challenging tasks conveys salient evidence of enhanced competence" (p. 48, 1989).

Students with Low Global Self-Concept were also found to show a significantly greater gain ($p < .01$) in Academic Self-Concept than students with High Global Self-Concept. Marsh and Richards (1988) found significant gains in Academic Self-Concept in their study of 66 low achieving high school males. Other authors have argued that outdoor adventure education courses would have no effect on Academic Self-Concept (Gillis, 1981). However, Hattie et al. (1997) note that the improvement of Academic Self-Concept is often not a primary or stated goal of outdoor adventure education programs (e.g., Outward Bound). The outdoor adventure education program at Friends Seminary is an academic class in which the students receive a grade. Students are required to make an oral presentation about any topic related to outdoor adventure education to a group, write a paper, and pass quizzes. Success in the outdoor adventure education classes may have a spillover effect to other classes, particularly in the area of strengthened problem solving ability (Hattie, et al.). Increased Social and Competence Self-Concept may contribute to increased Academic Self-Concept, as the domains of self-concept are moderately intercorrelated with one another (Bracken, 1992).

Outdoor adventure education activities appear to benefit students with High Global Self-Concept as well. Significant positive gains in Family Self-Concept were found for this group. Social interaction with other students, and the development of positive group experience may support and foster increased Family Self-Concept in students with High Global Self-Concept. Feelings of acceptance by peers, and the establishment of an identity associated with a peer group through interactions with others is an important developmental task during adolescence. Recreation activities, including outdoor adventure education experiences, allow adolescents to experiment with various identities (Grossman & O'Connell, 2000). The establishment and confirmation of an adolescent's identity of choice in the context of outdoor adventure education experiences may lead to an increase in Family Self-Concept by the recognition and support of that identity by a peer group. This may allow an easier transference of this and other identities to the family context, as adolescents not only recognize the reality of their identity, but conceptualize possible identities as well (Adamson & Lyxell, 1996).

In this study, high school students enrolled in outdoor adventure education courses categorized as having High Global Self-Concept showed greater gains in Physical Self-Concept. The physical nature of outdoor adventure education programs may reinforce existing positive thoughts regarding Physical Self-Concept, especially for students who already have high self-concept. Hattie et al. (1997) suggested increased Physical Self-Concept resulted from the realization of increased physical fitness upon return from an outdoor adventure education experience. They postulated that a change in reference group from others engaged in the outdoor experience (i.e., peers with the same physical abilities and experiences) to a convenient, everyday reference group (i.e., peers who were perceived to have inferior physical ability) led to an increase in Physical Self-Concept. The capability to conceptualize increased physical ability in different situations and use of a reference group that is perceived to have poorer physical ability may result in increased Physical Self-Concept, especially for students with High Global Self-Concept enrolled in outdoor adventure education courses.

Covariates

The lack of use of covariates in outdoor adventure education research has been identified as a weakness of previous studies (Hattie et al., 1997). This study collected information from participants for potential use as covariates in the repeated measures analysis of covariance (ANCOVA).

The lack of significant correlations between Perceived Risk of Outdoor Activities, Previous Level of Outdoor Experience, and Risk Taking Behaviors resulted in the elimination of these variables as covariates in all but one analysis. This indicates the suggestion of Hattie et al. (1997), who recommended future research include variables that may affect the dependent variable under study, need to be examined to a much greater extent. The identification and use of covariates such as self-efficacy, coping mechanisms, activity type, and intensity of experience may be more viable for use in future studies.

The results of this study address several areas of concern identified by previous researchers (Hattie et al., 1997; Neill, 1997). This study provides a reference point for outdoor adventure education courses offered in traditional high school academic settings, which have become increasingly popular. The fact that the program studied was not related to Outward Bound is another positive aspect, as it provides evidence of the effects of these types of programs in a different context. Outward Bound programs are generally characterized by long-term (14 to 21 day) experiences while programs such as the one studied emphasize a much shorter (two, three-day) experience. Other components of these programs are generally congruent with one another (e.g., backcountry setting, element of challenge, and small group size). The findings of this study thus may be generalized to other programs of similar nature.

This study provides evidence of the effectiveness of short-term outdoor adventure education courses for service providers, education administrators, and parents. Although increased self-concept may not be a stated benefit of particular programs, the outcomes of this research confirm enhanced high school student self-concept as a result of participating in outdoor adventure education courses. Administrators and program coordinators, many of who have been asked to shorten outdoor experiences as a result of lack of monetary resources and increased demands on student time, should note the results of this study. The nature of the courses studied (i.e., short-term, academic program) and the resultant changes in self-concept are of particular note. Additionally, the findings supporting increases in the various domains of self-concept for students characterized as having Low Global Self-Concept should be recognized. These increases may be "hidden" when students with both High and Low Global Self-Concept are considered together. The continued inclusion, expansion, or implementation of outdoor adventure education courses in private high school settings is supported by the research. Those offering outdoor adventure education experiences in similar settings should be aware of some of the factors that may affect change in high school student self-concept. The combination of outdoor adventure education activities, nature of the student/leader relationship, and length and number of outdoor experiences should be kept in mind when considering outcomes of participation.

Limitations

There are several limitations to this study. First, the use of a convenience sample limits the generalizability of the findings. This study employed high school students from a private school in New York City as participants. Related to this, most of the students were predominately Caucasian and by nature of a private school, of middle or upper middle socioeconomic class. Additionally, most students reported having grades of "B" or higher, generally indicating above-average scholastic ability. Many of these students previously knew each other as well. These factors may have played a role in the level of student self-concept, and how self-concept was affected by enrollment in outdoor adventure education courses. These findings may only be generalized to programs of this nature in large, urban environments. They should not be generalized to suburban or rural settings. A strength of this study was a generally equal number of male and female participants.

The researcher was unable to randomly assign participants to either the experimental or comparison group. However, there was no methodical process used by the school administration to assign tenth grade students to the fall semester outdoor adventure education courses. Broad scheduling factors were the only factor in determining which semester tenth grade students would take the outdoor adventure education course. Upper class students voluntarily enrolled in the outdoor adventure education course (i.e., Wilderness). This also affected the ability of the researcher to randomly assign student to the comparison or experimental group. These students were interested in furthering their outdoor experience and knowledge, potentially affecting how outdoor adventure education courses may impact on their self-concept, as these students may have higher self-concepts than those who did not enroll in this class.

Another limitation regards the activities in which students enrolled in the outdoor adventure education courses participated. Students in the Experiential Education class went on a rock climbing and winter camping trip, whereas the Wilderness class went on a sea kayaking and winter camping trip. Perhaps the difference in activity had an effect on change, or lack of change, in student self-concept. The rock climbing experience was of shorter duration and intensity than the sea kayaking experience. Students who rock climbed generally spent only 10 to 15 minutes per attempt actually climbing. Each student was given the opportunity to climb multiple times. When not climbing, students were either belaying (managing the safety rope) or providing support for the climbers. Students who went sea kayaking were engaged in the experience for a longer duration (up to 5 hours).

In addition, the rock climbers could choose between climbs with varying degrees of difficulty. The students who went sea kayaking were unable to choose the difficulty of the activity, as such factors as waves and wind were uncontrollable. The engagement in both rock climbing and sea kayaking is oriented to individual participation with support from other group members. The winter camping components of these courses were aimed more towards the group experience. The differences between the rock climbing and sea kayaking components of the outdoor adventure education courses may have affected the findings of this study.

The sample size of 94 students was adequate for statistical power as suggested by Cohen (1988). The retention of nearly all of the participants for the three waves of data collection is a strength of this study. However, a larger sample size using the same conditions may provide different results.

The timing of the waves of data collection may also have affected the findings of this study. The final wave of data collection occurred directly before the traditional holiday season school recess, which may have affected student self-concept. The stress of being engaged in school, increased workload (e.g., homework), studying for exams, and preparation of college applications by seniors make this a busy time of the academic year. Additionally, this final data collection was immediately after the outdoor component of these classes ended. Perhaps delaying the final data collection session would have allowed students to more fully integrate their experiences into their self-concept, and done so at a less busy time of the year.

Other aspects of outdoor activities such as weather, temperature, contact with other groups, and traffic to and from the location of the activity were not under control of the researcher. Additionally, the interpersonal relationships between the leaders and the students may have been different among groups. Generally, the rock climbing trips associated with the Experiential Education course had a larger ratio of students to leaders, while the Wilderness course had a smaller ratio of students to leaders. Although the factors mentioned above are also limitations for this research, the group leaders reported no untoward effects.

Recommendations

This researcher found both support and refutation of the findings of previous studies examining self-concept and outdoor adventure education with adolescents. The findings of this study regarding differences in change in self-concept between student with High and Low Global Self-Concept who were enrolled in outdoor adventure education courses warrant further research. Specifically, investigation into how and why outdoor adventure education programs differently affect students of various levels of self-concept is needed. Future research should identify and use covariates and other variables that may affect self-concept, especially for those students with low self-concept.

Outdoor adventure education courses with longer outdoor components have been shown to have more positive effects than short-term experiences (Hattie, et al., 1997). However, the findings of this study suggest there are some benefits of multiple short-term courses. Additional research is needed to clarify this issue. Factors such as length of time between short-term experiences, "timing" of the outdoor components in terms of their location in the greater academic schedule (e.g., Are the trips conducted during a busy time of the semester?), and the effects of the quantity of outdoor trips taken should be examined. The longitudinal effects of participation in these programs have received little attention. Further research in this area is needed.

Research should also be conducted using non-private school students. There may be latent factors affecting private high school students' self-concept that may be different from that of non-private school students. Studies should also examine programs offered by schools not located in large, urban environments.

This study did not examine the effects of the leadership team on changes in student self-concept. Future studies should include measurements of the leadership style(s) of the team members as well as the students' perceptions of their competencies and visions of them as outdoor leaders. Another aspect of leadership could be the students' expectations and perceptions of the leaders as role models compared to their actual experiences.

Another aspect of leadership may be the gender of the leaders. Having an all male or all female leadership team may affect change in self-concept, especially in same gender or in mixed gender groups. Additionally, the effects of continuous exposure to the leadership team both in and out of the traditional classroom over the course of the semester were not examined, and may be a factor. Perhaps exposure to new people in leadership roles would have a different effect on student self-concept.

Additionally, further research is needed as to the effects of participating in outdoor adventure education programs with single or mixed gender groups. Perhaps there are some gender related factors that may emerge in single gender groups that did not appear in this study.

Finally, although several researchers have investigated this topic, continual examination of change in self-concept as a result of participation in outdoor recreation activities should occur. The nature of the adolescent experience is ever changing. Increased exposure to electronic media, decreased levels of participation in physical activities, increased perceived level of daily stress, and the phenomenon of "growing up at a younger age" affect youth in contemporary society in much different ways than they did ten to fifteen years ago.

BIBLIOGRAPHY

Adamson, L. & Lyxell, B. (1996). Self-concept and questions of life: Identity development during late adolescence. Journal of Adolescence, 19, 569-582.

Archambault, F. (1995). Review of the Multidimensional Self Concept Scale. In J.C. Conoley & J.C. Impara (Eds.), The Twelfth Mental Measurements Yearbook (pp. 647-648). Lincoln, NE: University of Nebraska Press.

Aries, E., Olver, R., Blount, K., Christaldi, K., Fredman, S., & Lee, T. (1998). Race and gender as components of the working self-concept. The Journal of Social Psychology, 138 (3), 277-290.

Bandura, A. (1977). Self efficacy: Toward a unifying theory of behavioral change. Psychological Review, 84, 191-215.

Beane, J. A., & Lipka, R. P. (1980). Self-concept and self-esteem: A construct differentiation. Child Study Journal, 10 (1), 1-6.

Bracken, B. (1992). Multidimensional Self Concept Scale. Austin, TX: PRO-ED, Inc.

Bracken, B. (Ed.). (1996). Handbook of Self-Concept. New York: John Wiley & Sons.

Bracken, B., Bunch, S., Keith, T., & Keith, P. (2000). Child and adolescent multidimensional self-concept: A five-instrument factor analysis. Psychology in the Schools, 37, (6), 483-493.

Bracken, B., & Howell, K. (1991) Multidimensional self concept validation: A three-instrument investigation. Journal of Psychoeducational Assessment, 9, 319-328.

Bracken, B., & Mills, B. (1994, September). School counselors' assessment of self-concept: A comprehensive review of 10 instruments. The School Counselor, 42, 14-31.

Brown, J.D., & Siegel, J.M. (1988). Exercise as a buffer of life stress: A prospective study of adolescent health. Health Psychology, 7 (4), 341-353.

Byrne, B.M. (1984). The general/academic self-concept nomological network: A review of construct validation research. Review of Educational Research, 54, 427-456.

Byrne, B.M. (1996). Measuring self-concept across the life span: Issues and instrumentation. Washington, D.C.: American Psychological Association.

Byrne, B.M., & Shavelson, R.J. (1987). Adolescent self-concept: Testing the assumption of equivalent structure across gender. American Educational Research Journal, 24 (3), 365-385.

Cason, D. & Gillis, H.L. (1994). A meta-analysis of outdoor adventure programming with adolescents. The Journal of Experiential Education, 17 (1), 40-47.

Cohen, J. (1988). Statistical power analysis for the behavioral sciences. Hillsdale, NJ: Lawrence Erlbaum Associates.

Cooley, C.H. (1902). Human nature and the social order. New York: Charles Scribner's Sons.

Crain, R. (1996). The influence of age, race, and gender on child and adolescent multidimensional self-concept. In B. Bracken (Ed.), Handbook of Self-Concept. New York: John Wiley & Sons, Inc.

Crain, R., & Bracken, B. (1994). Age, race, and gender differences in child and adolescent self-concept: Evidence from a behavioral-acquisition, context-dependent model. School Psychology Review, 23 (3), 496-516.

Csikszentmihalyi, M. (1975). Beyond boredom and anxiety. San Francisco: Jossey-Bass.

Delugach, R., Bracken, B., Bracken, M.J., & Schicke, M. (1992, July). Self-concept: Multidimensional construct exploration. Psychology in the Schools, 29, 213-223.

Ewert, A. (1983). Outdoor adventure and self-concept: A research analysis Eugene: University of Oregon, Center of Leisure Studies.

Ewert, A. (1987). Emerging trends in outdoor adventure recreation. In J. Meier, T. Morash, & G. Welton (Eds.), High-adventure outdoor pursuits: Organization and leadership. (pp. 149-159). Columbus, OH: Publishing Horizons, Inc.

Ewert, A. (1989). Outdoor adventure pursuits: Foundations, models, and theories. Columbus, OH: Publishing Horizons, Inc.

Finkenberg, M., Shows, D., & DiNucci, J. (1994). Participation in adventure-based activities and self-concepts of college men and women. Perceptual and Motor Skills, 78, 1119-1122.

Gillett, D., Thomas, G., Skok, R., & McLaughlin, T. (1991). The effects of wilderness camping and hiking on the self-concept and the environmental attitudes and knowledge of twelfth graders. Journal of Environmental Education, 22 (3), 33-43.

Gillis, H.L. (1981). The effects of camping/construction experience on the self-concepts, locus of control, and academic achievement of high school students. Unpublished master's thesis, Middle Tennessee State University.

Grossman, A. & O'Connell, T. (2000). In M.C. Cabeza (Ed.), Leisure and human development (pp. 187-192). Bilbao, Spain: University of Deusto.

Harter, S. (1986). Processes underlying the construction, maintenance, and enhancement of the self-concept of children. In J. Suls & A. G. Greenwald (Eds.), Psychological perspectives on the self: Vol. 3 (pp. 137-181). Hillsdale, NJ: Lawrence Erlbaum Associates.

Hattie, J. (1992). Self-Concept. Hillsdale, NJ: Lawrence Erlbaum Associates.

Hattie, J., Marsh, H., Neill, J., & Richards, G. (1997). Adventure education and Outward Bound: Out-of-class experiences that make a lasting difference. Review of Educational Research, 67 (1), 43-87.

Hazelworth, M., & Wilson, B. (1990). The effects of an outdoor adventure camp experience on self-concept. Journal of Environmental Education, 21 (4), 33-37.

Iso-Ahola, S. (1976). On the theoretical link between personality and leisure. Psychological Reports, 39, 3-10.

Jackson, L., Hodge, C., & Ingram, J. (1994). Gender and self-concept: A reexamination of stereotypic differences and the role of gender attitudes. Sex Roles, 30 (9/10), 615-630.

James, W. (1983). Principles of psychology, (Vol. 1). Cambridge, MA: Harvard University Press. (Original work published 1890).

Kaplan, R. (1974). Some psychological benefits of an outdoor challenge program. Environment and Behavior, 6 (1), 101-116.

Kimmel, D.C., & Weiner, I.B. (1995). Adolescence: A developmental transition (second edition). New York: John Wiley & Sons.

Lambert, M.J., Segger, J.F., Staley, J.S., Spencer, B., & Nelson, D. (1978). Reported self-concept and self-actualizing value changes as a function of academic classes with wilderness experience. Perceptual and Motor Skills, 46, 1035-1040.

Leonard, N.H., Beauvais, L.L., & Scholl, R.W. (1995). Self-concept based motivation [On-line]. Available: http://www.cba.uri.edu/scholl/notes/self_concept_model.html

Lewis, C.E., Siegel, J.M., & Lewis, M.A. (1984). Feeling bad: Exploring the sources of distress among pre-adolescent children. American Journal of Public Health, 74, 117-122.

Luckner, J. (1989). Effects of participation in an outdoor adventure education course on the self-concept of hearing-impaired individuals. American Annals of the Deaf, 134, (1), 45-49.

Marsh, H.W. (1989). Age and sex effects in multiple dimensions of self-concept: Preadolescence to early adulthood. Journal of Educational Psychology, 81 (3), 417-430.

Marsh, H.W. (1993). The multidimensional structure of academic self-concept: invariance over gender and age. American Educational Research Journal, 30 (4), 841-860.

Marsh, H.W., & Hattie, J. (1996). Theoretical perspectives on the structure of self-concept. In B. Bracken (Ed.), Handbook of self-concept (pp. 38-90). John Wiley & Sons: New York.

Marsh, H. W., Parker, J., & Barnes, J. (1985). Multidimensional adolescent self-concepts: Their relationship to age, sex, and academic measures. American Educational Research Journal, 22 (3), 422-444.

Marsh, H.W., & Richards, G.E. (1988). The Outward Bound Bridging Course for low-achieving high school males: Effect on academic achievement and multidimensional self-concept. Australian Journal of Psychology, 40 (3), 281-298.

Marsh, H.W., Richards, G.E., & Barnes, J. (1986). Multidimensional self-concepts: The effects of participation in an Outward Bound program. Journal of Personality and Social Psychology, 50 (1), 195-204.

Marsh, H.W., Richards, G.E., & Barnes, J. (1987). Multidimensional self-concepts: A long-term follow-up of the effect of participation in an Outward Bound program. Personality and Social Psychology Bulletin, 12 (4), 475-492.

Marsh, H.W., & Shavelson, R. (1985). Self-concept: Its multifaceted, hierarchical structure. Educational Psychologist, 20 (3), 107-123.

Marx, R.W., & Winne, P.H. (1980). Self-concept validation research: Some current complexities. Measurement and Evaluation in Guidance, 13, 72-82.

McDonald, R., & Howe, C. (1989). Challenge/initiative recreation programs for low self-concept children. Journal of Leisure Research, 21 (3), 242-253.

Minor, K., & Elrod, P. (1994). The effects of a probation intervention on juvenile offenders' self-concepts, loci of control, and perceptions of juvenile justice. Youth and Society, 25 (4), 490-511.

Neill, J. (1997, January). Outdoor education in the schools: What can it achieve? Paper presented at the 10th National Outdoor Education Conference, Sydney, Australia.

Priest, S. (1993). A new model for risk taking. The Journal of Experiential Education, 16 (1), 50-53.

Purkey, W. (1988). An overview of self-concept theory for counselors. Ann Arbor, MI: Clearinghouse on Counseling and Personnel Services. (ERIC/CAPS Digest No. ED 304 630).

Rawson, H. & McIntosh, D. (1991, April). Does camping really lead to changes in self-esteem? Camping Magazine, 18-21.

Rosenberg, M. (1986). Self-concept from middle childhood through adolescence. In J. Suls & A. G. Greenwald (Eds.), Psychological perspectives on the self: Vol. 3 (pp. 107-136). Hillsdale, NJ: Lawrence Erlbaum Associates.

Rotatori, A. (1994, January). Test review: Multidimensional Self-Concept Scale. Measurement and Evaluation in Counseling and Development, 26, 265-268.

Rothenberg, D. (1995). Supporting girls in early adolescence. Urbana, IL: Clearinghouse on Elementary and Early Childhood Education. (ERIC Digest No. ED 386 331).

Shavelson, R., Hubner, J., & Stanton, G. (1976). Self-concept: Validation of construct interpretations. Review of Educational Research, 46 (3), 407-441.

Stake, J.E., (1992). Gender differences and similarities in self-concept within everyday life contexts. Psychology of Women Quarterly, 16, 349-363.

Strein, W. (1998). Assessment of self-concept. Greensboro, NC: Clearinghouse on Counseling and Student Services. (ERIC Digest No. Ed 389 962 95).

Tabachnick, B. & Fidell, L. (1996). Using Multivariate Statistics. New York: Harper Collins College Publishers.

Widaman, K., MacMillan, D., Hemsley, R., Little, T., & Balow, I. (1992). Differences in adolescents' self-concept as a function of academic level, ethnicity, and gender. American Journal of Mental Retardation, 96 (4), 387-404.

Wilgenbush, T., & Merrell, K. (1999). Gender differences in self-concept among children and adolescents: A meta-analysis of multidimensional studies. School Psychology Quarterly, 14 (2), 101-120.

Willis, W.G. (1995). Review of the Multidimensional Self Concept Scale. In J.C. Conoley & J.C. Impara (Eds.), The Twelfth Mental Measurements Yearbook (pp. 648-650). Lincoln, NE: University of Nebraska Press.

Young, A. & Ewert, A. (1992). Fear in outdoor education: The influence of gender and program. In K. Henderson, (Ed.), Proceedings of the CEO Outdoor Education Research Symposium (pp. 83-90). Cortland, NY: Coalition for Education in the Outdoors.

Printed by
Schaltungsdienst Lange o.H.G., Berlin